The Revisionists Revised

THE
REVISIONISTS
REVISED

A CRITIQUE OF
THE RADICAL ATTACK
ON THE SCHOOLS

DIANE RAVITCH

Basic Books, Inc., Publishers   New York

Portions of this book appeared in different form in *The American Scholar* 46, no. 2 (Spring 1977). Copyright © 1977 by the United Chapters of Phi Beta Kappa. Reprinted by permission.

Library of Congress Cataloging in Publication Data

Ravitch, Diane.
  The revisionists revised.

  Includes bibliographical references and index.
  1.   Education—United States—History—Sources.
I.   Title.
LA212.R36   1978   370'.973   77-20417
ISBN: 0-465-06943-6

For *Anna* and *David Silverstein* of Lumzar, Poland,

and Savannah, Georgia;

and for *Bertha* and *Gerson Katz* of Balti, Bessarabia,

and Houston, Texas;

Who knew why they came and never forgot.

And for *Anna* and *Walter "Cracker" Silvers*

of Houston, Texas;

Who remembered and understood.

CONTENTS

CONTENTS

PREFACE

AMERICAN attitudes towards formal education are paradoxical. There is, on the one hand, abundant evidence of a deep commitment to education, if commitment can be measured by numbers of participants and dollars. In the fall of 1975, for example, some 70 million Americans were enrolled in formal educational programs; 44.8 million of these were students in public elementary and secondary schools. About $120 billion was spent on education in 1975, two-thirds of it for public elementary and secondary schools, nearly 8 percent of the United States gross national product—more than was spent on either national defense or health. Every American community makes a substantial contribution of its local taxes to support schools for its young.

Yet, on the other hand, this munificently endowed activity is usually caught between public moods of apathy and hostility. Unless there is a controversy to stir interest, public attitudes towards educational issues seem to range from dissatisfaction to disinterest. Periodically, educational institutions are the object of scathing attacks from left, right, and center; from students, teachers, and parents; from business and labor; from the media; and even, to judge by reports that stream from foundations and commissions, from its own leaders. At any one time, there are those who claim that the schools spend too much and those who claim that they spend too little; those who would abolish all standardized tests and those who would impose statewide, even nationwide, standardized tests; those who demand that everyone get a college education and those who complain that the colleges are accepting unqualified students. Since Americans don't agree on what they expect of schools, they can't agree on whether the schools respond to criticism too slowly or too quickly.

Typically, the critics divide into two groups: those who think that the schools can do much more and much better and those who think that they are trying to do far more than they can possibly accomplish. No matter how strenuously they criticize the schools, both sides implicitly accept the usefulness and importance and permanence of the institution of schooling, even though they may not admire it in its present form. Indeed, their complaints are directed to the end of making the schools better.

A different strain of criticism achieved prominence during the 1960s and 1970s. The new critics—radical critics—directly challenged the usefulness of schooling and questioned not whether Americans had placed too much faith in education, but why they had placed *any* faith in education.

Now, one of the great attractions of a free society is the prospect of a good debate, and one would have expected that the radical critics of education, having flayed one of the nation's most sacred cows, would encounter vigorous rebuttals. But, oddly, this was not the case. Perhaps educational leaders were painfully aware of the flaws of their enterprise, but for whatever reason, the good debate between educational radicals and educational liberals has not taken place. In my own field of educational history, radical historians have encountered little opposition; even books which, in my view, flagrantly violated the rules of evidence and logic went unchallenged. Scholars who disagreed profoundly chose to look the other way rather than engage in controversy with the radical historians. One prominent historian wrote, in response to an early version of this book, that he agreed with what I had written but had been afraid to state the same things himself; another historian wrote that he now realized that his error in the 1960s was in keeping silent for fear of being shouted down. I hope that the present book will contribute to the lively debate that American education needs at all times.

In the fall of 1975, the National Academy of Education invited me to review the works of the radical historians of education. I had already written reviews of some of them and was delighted to have the opportunity to consider the radical historians as a group. I presented my major findings at a meeting of the Academy in May 1976, and the review was published by the Academy in February 1977. Basic Books, which had published two of the works reviewed as well as my own previous book, asked me to expand the 84-page essay, and the present work is the result. Brief portions of this book appeared previously in *The American Scholar* and *Teachers College Record*; both publications have kindly granted permission to reprint these excerpts.

There are many people to whom I am deeply indebted. I wish to thank those who read early drafts of the manuscript and gave me their comments, criticisms, and disagreements: J. Freeman Butts, Lawrence A. Cremin, David

L. Featherman, Rita Kramer, David Tyack, Wayne J. Urban, and Rush Welter. I wish to express my gratitude to the National Academy of Education, to its then president, Patrick Suppes, and its executive secretary, William D. Hyde, Jr. for their patience during the editorial process and for permission to adapt the original essay into its present form. It is the three most important people in my life to whom I owe the most—my sons, Joey and Michael, and my husband, Richard—for it is they who make possible the delicate balancing act that permits me to function simultaneously as wife, mother, scholar, and writer. Lastly, this book is dedicated to my grandparents and parents, who would have found it difficult to comprehend the issues raised in the following pages.

DIANE RAVITCH

The Revisionists Revised

CHAPTER ONE

The Democratic-Liberal Tradition Under Attack

Dᴜʀɪɴɢ the past decade or so, the democratic-liberal tradition in American education has come under sharp attack, particularly from radical critics. In dozens of books and articles, radical writers have charged that American educational institutions have not played the democratic, benevolent role that educators have traditionally claimed for them. On the contrary, assert these critics, the schools are themselves oppressive institutions which regiment, indoctrinate, and sort children, either brutally or subtly crushing their individuality and processing them to take their place in an unjust social order. Indeed, say these critics, the major function of the schools is to mask the "oppressive" features of an undemocratic society.

Criticism of the schools, radical or otherwise, is nothing new. In every generation the schools have had vociferous critics. Religious leaders have complained either that the schools were morally neutral and therefore irreligious, or that they covertly advanced the interests of one sect over another. Political groups have condemned the schools either because they failed to inculcate patriotism or pacifism, or because they were indoctrinating children to a particular political perspective. Conservatives have denounced the schools both for their extravagance and their egalitarian pretensions. Radicals have long dismissed the schools as a tool of the capitalist economy which distracts attention from the need for fundamental change. And liberals have perennially despaired of ever getting enough money, skilled personnel, and public support to make the schools achieve their full potential as a mechanism to promote both individual development and social equality. As Richard Hofstadter observed, the history of educational commentary in America is "a literature of acid criticism and bitter complaint."[1]

In every society there is an integral, reciprocal relationship between education and politics; the kind of education available (however broadly it is defined) influences the nature of politics and society, just as the nature of politics and society has a determinative effect on educational policy. Nations that rule by coercion require citizens who have been educated to accept coercion. A free society, committed to popular rule, must provide an education that prepares people to think for themselves and to function as free citizens. In its basic values, the democratic-liberal tradition argues for an education that respects the worth and dignity of each individual, that prizes freedom of inquiry and expression, and that enables each person to think and participate and choose independently. Just as freedom of religion is safeguarded by the multiplicity of religious groups in America, so freedom of thought is protected by the plurality of the sources of education and information—not limited to schools—and by the diversity of those who control the various agencies of education, whether public or private.

In recent years, the democratic-liberal tradition has been subject to distortion by some who think of themselves as liberals. It seems worthwhile, therefore, to delineate some of these misconceptions: It is not necessarily "liberal" to spend ever greater amounts of money on education without regard to effectiveness or quality; it is not necessarily "liberal" to transfer power from the private sector to the public sector without concern for the potential increase of bureaucratization, standardization, and coercion in American life; it is not necessarily "liberal" to advocate greater governmental regulation of family and community life. It is not easy to reconcile the often conflicting needs of the collectivity and the individual or to maintain a healthy balance between the private sector and the public sector. Yet a liberal democracy must maintain its commitments both to social welfare and to the preeminence of free institutions and individual liberties.

In terms of school policy, the programmatic implications of the democratic-liberal tradition have been gradually, if imperfectly, embodied in practice. If universal education is essential to a democratic society, then schooling should be not only universal, but free, publicly supported, and equally available to all. If talent and intelligence are randomly distributed throughout society, then schools must serve as a means for individuals to develop their fullest potential without regard to race, sex, religion, or other ascriptive factors. Liberals have maintained that equal opportunity in education would prevent the hardening of class lines and facilitate social mobility; that education broadly available would stimulate general progress as well as individual mobility; that only popular education makes possible the formation of a common culture, accessible to all; that political participation is stimulated by the dispersion of education, and politics becomes more democratic as more people participate by creating new publics to express their interests; and, that the freest possible exercise of human reason would contribute to the establishment of a good society. The democratic-liberal theory of education is, then, simultaneously a theory of society, a theory of politics, and a theory of culture.

Conservatives have reacted negatively to this tradition because of its implicit egalitarianism. Education had been associated in Europe with aristocratic privilege, and there was more than rhetoric in the saying that knowledge is power. The suspicion lingered that education spreads discontent, envy, and an unquenchable thirst for equality. On the other hand, radicals have attacked the democratic-liberal tradition precisely because it was not sufficiently egalitarian. Equal opportunity is not the same as equal results, and to radicals, equal opportunity means meritocracy, which they find as reprehensible as aristocracy.

These polar reactions have each had a floodtide in recent decades. Conservative criticism reached a zenith in the 1950s, when opponents of progressive education demanded the elimination of "fads and frills," as well as the purging of "internationalist" and "socialist" influences, from the public schools' curricula. Educational radicalism became popular in the 1960s, as radical critics assailed the central tenets of liberalism. The schools, they charged, were rigid, repressive institutions whose real purpose was to preserve the social order by inculcating passivity and conformity. Some scorned the idea of public schooling and urged countercultural "free" schools instead, while others rejected institutionalized schooling altogether. The radicals raised questions that had seemingly been long settled: Is compulsory schooling a denial of children's liberty? Do adults have the right to impose their values on the younger generation? What is the moral basis for authority in the classroom? Are all educational standards arbitrary? Is schooling simply a sociological cookie-cutter, coercing children into a common mold and readying them for the industrial needs of the capitalist economy?

Underlying such questions is a fundamental divergence between liberals and radicals about the direction of American history. Recalling the reciprocal relationship between education and society, it becomes clear that any scheme of deliberate education represents a choice on the part of the educator, a commitment to a particular view of society. Liberals tend to believe that American society has become more open, more inclusive, and more democratic over time, not accidentally or inevitably, but because of political action by those who sought these goals. Thus, if one believes in the values of a free, democratic society and prefers rational persuasion to coercion, then one must teach what those values mean and how to function in such a society. Radicals, however, tend to believe that the basic trend in American history has been a straight line—unremittingly racist, bureaucratic, exclusive, and undemocratic. Influenced largely by economic determinism, radicals perceive "vested interests" so powerful that no change can take place unless it is sponsored by those interests. Given this understanding, political action is fruitless because it can occur only if it is ineffectual. Educational reform, in this view, merely buttresses an unjust political system by making it operate more efficiently and flexibly.

Since the consequences of any particular change are never entirely predictable, reformers must be risk-takers. When they are effective, reformers become responsible for the changes they institute. And when, at some future date, the reforms need reforming, their original sponsors can be disparaged for not having had the prescience to see what would go wrong. Thus, anyone who gets involved in political action runs the considerable risk of failing, while those who refuse to abandon their utopian ideals never can be held accountable. The liberal reformer who wants to bring about incremental change must negotiate with those who oppose him and, in doing so, may have to compromise some of his original commitment. The radical preserves the purity of his principles by remaining aloof from the system and from any ultimate responsibility for its success or failure. By definition, then, the reformer is one who grapples with political and social problems and seeks solutions, while the radical eschews entanglement with a "corrupt" system, since any incremental improvement would only help secure the social order. And again by definition, anyone who participates politically is predestined to be corrupted, to be a "servant of power," and thus to fail when judged by radical standards.

The democratic-liberal tradition in education has been bound up with the spirit of reform, a sense that education could be consciously arranged to make American society more open, more just, and more democratic. This view has been persistently misrepresented by radical critics to mean that liberals saw the schools as a universal panacea and devoted energies to school reform that should have been directed to economic and social change. Indeed, the radical historians assert that the liberal's promotion of schooling was *intended* to divert attention from more salient issues. This is not, however, a fair reading of the liberal position, at least as it has been expressed by its leading exponents. Thomas Jefferson, certainly no advocate of the school as a universal panacea, wrote clearly about the interconnectedness of the institutions of a free society, and free schools were no more important (indeed, were rather less important) in his concept than a free press and a democratic polity. Though Horace Mann passionately advanced the cause of the public schools (which was scarcely surprising since he was employed by the state of Massachusetts to do so), he was also active on behalf of prison reform, better treatment for the insane, temperance legislation, and abolition. If his faith in the power of schooling now seems naive and excessive, it is a judgment made possible by hindsight. Merle Curti held that

Mann should not be judged harshly for overemphasizing the ameliorating role of education. Confidence in the efficacy of the school as a means of effecting social change was then in its heyday. Education on a large scale had not been tried for a sufficiently long time to disprove his belief that it would vanquish crime, the excesses of profit-making, and even poverty itself. Finally, the unqualified acceptance of education as a means of remedying social evils was the natural corollary to the dominant belief in individualism which Mann, like almost everyone else, shared.

9

Like Mann, John Dewey believed that the schools, rightly conceived and organized, might become a lever of social progress, but he did not see the school as the *sole* instrument of social and economic change. It was, he maintained, a necessary though not a sufficient condition in the creation of a better social order. And in the late 1930s, he warned that the schools, as they became more pervasive and efficient, could become instruments controlled by a totalitarian state, as they had in Nazi Germany. He was himself a critic of the naive and simplistic faith in the public schools' automatic goodness:

after a century of belief that the Common School system was bound by the very nature of its work to be what its earlier apostles called a 'pillar of the republic', we are learning that everything about the public schools, its official agencies of control, organization and administration, the status of teachers, the subjects taught and methods of teaching them, the prevailing modes of discipline, set *problems*; and that the problems have been largely ignored as far as the relation of schools to democratic institutions is concerned.

So much attention had been lavished on the technical side of school questions, he complained, that "the central question"—the relation of schools to democratic institutions—had been obscured.[2]

Schooling, though not necessarily public schooling, was recognized by liberal thinkers as one of the cultural conditions that would nurture a free, democratic society. Schooling was a means, political and social democracy the end. That liberal aspirations have not been fully realized (and have even occasionally been negated) is not an indictment of the aspiration but is rather an acknowledgment of the difficulty of the goal and the stubbornness of human nature and institutions. To be sure, to define the ideal is to become aware of the distance between ideal and practice, though the appropriate analytical question is not whether there is a gap between ideal and practice, but whether the gap is growing larger or smaller. Nonetheless, the ideal remains, even when imperfectly realized, a standard by which to measure practice. The lapses from the standard are all the more conspicuous because they are lapses, exceptions to educational aspirations which are broadly shared even when they are still unattained.

To recount the history of education strictly as an ideological struggle, in which certain seminal thinkers led the way, bringing educational reform in their wake, needlessly sharpens the contrast between rhetoric and reality while serving up a desiccated version of complicated events. There is never a simple cause-and-effect relationship between ideas and events. Men like Jefferson, Mann, and Dewey were not innovators as much as they were articulators of major trends, and their ideas form the mainstream of American educational thought because they correctly analyzed and identified the moving historical forces of their time. Jefferson's 1779 proposal for a pyramidal structure of public education was rejected by the Virginia legislature but eventually became the prototype of American public schooling, not because Jefferson said it should, but because it was what most nearly satisfied the wishes of voters, taxpayers, and legislators. Jefferson's concern for both equality and excellence turned out to have been an accurate prediction, though not necessarily a proximate cause, of the American public school system. Mann is known as the father of the common (public) school movement, but common schools were established in many towns and districts long before Mann became involved in the question. He was the best known advocate of a movement that was already well underway, not its progenitor. The movements with which Mann and Dewey were identified were not created by their pens, but by a confluence of forces within American society. Dewey influenced and inspired the progressive education movement, but he neither invented nor directed it. A comprehensive analysis of educational policy must include not only ideas and ideals but also consideration of the underlying political, economic, and social conditions that cause one set of ideas and not another to come to the fore. Recognizing this, Dewey argued against the reductionist tendency to locate single causes:

we have to get away from the influence of belief in bald single forces, whether they are thought of as intrinsically psychological or sociological. . . . We have to analyze conditions by observations, which are as discriminating as they are extensive, until we discover specific interactions that are taking place, and learn to think in terms of interactions instead of force. We are led to search even for the conditions which have given the interacting factors the power they possess.[3]

Those who attribute the spread of public schooling solely to Horace Mann's forcefulness, or to the organizing skills of other school reformers, underestimate the objective conditions that persuaded people in diverse communities to tax themselves on behalf of public schooling while prohibiting public funds for sectarian instruction. Sometimes nonsectarianism was simply anti-Catholicism, but it can also be seen as a compromise that permitted people of different sects, none in a majority, to school their children together. The effect of the common school revival in the mid-nineteenth century was to build support for state-enforced educational standards and to promote the cause of public schooling. The economist Albert Fishlow has noted that mass schooling was well established in the New England states by 1830, before the common school revival. Fishlow holds that Mann's activities were directed not merely against indifference to education, but also against a burgeoning of private and semiprivate educational activities. Because historians of education have largely been professional educators, with a special stake in public education, they have traditionally depicted Mann's fight for public schooling as a crusade of principle rather than as a genuine controversy between public and private interests, with a degree of right on both sides.[4]

The subsidiary effect of the common school movement was to formulate a powerful, sometimes evangelistic, ideology for the American public school. Mann was Jeffersonian in the sense that he clearly perceived the interrelationship among education, society, and politics. But unlike Jefferson, whose concept of a "crusade against ignorance" put no special emphasis on public schooling, Mann argued that the public school was uniquely suited to carry forward the promise of American life. He grounded his plea for the primacy of the common school on generally held assumptions about the beneficial power of education. But not everyone believed, as he did, that the fate of the nation was inextricably tied to the fate of public schools. The view that education was morally uplifting, that it improved character and prevented poverty and vice, was commonplace, in part because of the traditional association of religion and education, but also because of the empirical evidence: criminals and paupers were likelier than not to be unlettered. So reformers of Mann's era shared his belief in the power of universal education without necessarily adopting his commitment to public schooling. Governor William Seward of New York, as dedicated to social reform as Mann, urged public support for Catholic schools as a means of extending the blessings of education to the children of poor Irish Catholics who shunned the publicly supported nonsectarian schools of New York City. Despite their very different opinions about the necessity of common schooling, Mann and Seward both believed that unequal education was the basis of social inequality, and both believed that the state had an obligation to remedy the inequity. The area of agreement between these two contemporaries defines the popular values to which reformers appealed. As political leaders, Mann and Seward were anxious to persuade their publics to adopt their programs and took care to express their ideas in what they hoped would be a convincing fashion. In other words, they clothed their innovative proposals in popular rhetoric. Theirs was an optimistic, individualistic outlook. It said that anyone could overcome his original circumstances by his own effort, that a young man should have no bounds other than his own ability and energy. It assumed that heredity and authority counted for little and that American society ought to be open, democratic, and malleable. Though in some parts of the country blacks, women, and certain other minorities were excluded from participating as equals, the internal dynamic of this outlook contained the eventual destruction of these contradictions.

These were the values of a society bent on self-improvement, a society with fluid class lines, a society where Horatio Alger stories would become popular, a society

that would ultimately be compelled by its own democratic *Come on ?*
creed to confront its prejudices and discriminatory practices and seek to abolish them. In such a society, with its
emphasis on self-improvement and getting ahead, educational enterprises of all kinds thrived, not just schools, but
museums, libraries, Chautauquas, settlement houses, de-
bating societies, labor unions, political clubs, and count-
less other activities intended to teach, to learn, to change
people's minds or skills or values or sensibilities.

In the midst of all this educational busyness, the public
school assumed a special place, not because Mann and
other reformers said it should, but because it was there
that the rising generation would be systematically in-
structed. By the time of the Civil War, most American
children outside the South attended public schools. The
most important fact about the American public schools
was that they were popularly controlled. This meant that
school policy could not deviate very far from popular
dictates and that the schools would largely reflect the
aspirations and values of the polity, for better or worse.
Reformers might propose this or that change, but they had
to win the approval of the local school board, which was
either popularly elected or appointed by elected officials.
The financing of schools injected another political con-
straint, either through popular referenda or through the
legislative process.

Whatever the issue at hand, reformers had to take into
account the necessity of persuading others to agree with
them. In other nations, the schools were controlled by the
established church or by a powerful centralized state
agency. Popular control in the United States meant that
school politics was an extension of democratic politics. If

the public schools did not satisfy the voters, there were various ways by which their dissatisfaction might be expressed: by voting against the school board, by sending their children to nonpublic schools, by opposing a school bond issue, or by lobbying their elected representatives. The displeasure of a few irate parents might not cause a stir, but mass disaffection could not be ignored.

Because of the interconnection of the schools' politics with the politics of the society at large, the schools generally reflect the society. An electorate will not long support a school system that openly subverts its wishes, values, and interests. School policy usually represents what most people expect of schools at any particular time; a school board that tried to introduce changes that were repugnant to the community would not long survive so long as there were some mechanism of popular control. Because the demands made on them are simultaneously liberal and conservative, the schools are simultaneously liberal and conservative. Indeed, to the frustration of ideological purists, the distinction between that which is liberal and that which is conservative is not always clear, since most people are liberal in one sphere and conservative in another; it is not unusual, for example, to encounter individuals who are politically liberal and pedagogically conservative, as well as the reverse.

This curious intermingling of opposite impulses has been evidenced in other contexts. When Mann sought to persuade people to support public schools more generously, he appealed alternately to those who wanted a more equal society and to those who wanted a more stable society. He argued both that education would be a great equalizer and that it would disarm the poor of their hostility toward the rich. Part of the political potency of the public school idea in the United States has been this simultaneous appeal to disparate interests. The continuing strength of the schools is due to the fact that they have at least partially fulfilled the expectations of their differing constituencies.

This outcome, this blurring and compromising of conflicting demands, is the result of a political process which continually strives for conciliation and coalition-building, for settlements in which the victors are not totally victorious and the losers not totally vanquished. To be sure, this consensual political process is a manifestation of democratic, pluralist politics, in which many groups and individuals press for their own interests and arrive at a resolution which satisfies most of the participants and crushes none. Radicals, believing in the inexorability as well as the desirability of class struggle, see the political process as a way of defusing discontent without sharply altering the status quo.

The difference between them comes down to the radicals' exclusive preoccupation with ends as contrasted with the liberals' concern with means and ends in relation. Carl Becker wrote that "The case for democracy is that it accepts the rational and humane values as ends, and proposes as the means of realizing them the minimum of coercion and the maximum of voluntary assent." An anarchist society, if such a contradiction could exist, would have no compulsion whatever, and very likely have no means of assuring elementary standards of equity; a Marxist society, which places its emphasis on ends, tolerates the maximum of coercion in pursuing its goals. Fundamental to a democratic-liberal society is the recognition that basic values endure but are realized partially, incrementally, and sporadically; that ends and means are inseparable; that one ultimately determines the other, and that inhumane means can never produce humane ends.[5]

Educational politics is not simply a mirror image of the politics of the larger society, though many of the same values permeate both. It involves a wide array of interest groups—teachers, parents, supervisors, students, elected officials, state education agencies, federal officials, foundations, unions, good government groups, and the press. In any particular decision, the interested parties shift in terms of the intensity of their concern. But the process of decision-making—the impact of public opinion, the necessity of discussion and agreement, the negotiations among different constituencies, the constraints of law and the judiciary—is democratic.

To say that the policy process is democratic is not to say that every decision that comes forth is correct. Political solutions are often temporary, expedient, or short-sighted. In the short run, the test of educational policy is whether it works, whether it satisfies most participants, whether it assures majority rule without traducing the rights of the minority. There may be an objectively better way to do things, which may be obvious to those with the perspective of history; but unless the participants can be persuaded of the better way, then it will have to wait for another time, a time when its proponents are more effective in their role as educators of the public.

Because education is so bound up with the interests and values of the public, and because these interests and values continually shift over time, educational policy can never be static. It is forever in the process of becoming, forever a subject of proper concern, forever in need of reformulation. At some times in our history there has seemed to be a better fit between educational institutions and perceived needs than at other times, and the schools were said to be doing "a good job" and "meeting society's needs." But as American society changes, so must and do the schools. Change never comes easily. Generally, it occurs after much debate, agitation, complaint, and criticism; and it is in this perspective that the radical critics play a useful and important function by prodding educational policymakers to reexamine their assumptions, their intentions, and their effectiveness. To respond to criticism intelligently, without reinventing the wheel, without unknowingly re-enacting some cyclical drama, educational policymakers need to know the history of which they are a part. They need to understand the aspirations, the values, and the traditions that have shaped American education. They cannot have an adequate sense of the future without having an adequate sense of the past, nor can they judge what should be without knowing what has been.

CHAPTER TWO

Revisionist Trends

Two significant revisionist trends appeared in American historiography in the early 1960s. The first, inspired by Richard Hofstadter's *The Age of Reform*, was a re-evaluation of the progressive era, with all its troublesome and illiberal strains. This critical reconsideration of the progressive-liberal tradition, which had claimed the automatic loyalty of many historians, caused one historian to predict, with a sense of relief, "It now seems possible, at long last, to deal dispassionately with certain subjects which have been for decades hidden under a hard crust of political and ideological attachments." Henceforth, the historian would have to examine not just the bright, democratic side of progressivism, not just the reformers, the trustbusters, and the muckrakers, but also the elitist, antidemocratic underside as well, as embodied in, for example, the immigration restriction movement.[1]

The second trend, reflecting a growing impatience with
the pace of social change in the United States, undertook
not merely a reassessment of liberalism but a repudiation
of it. Referred to as radical revisionism, it outspokenly
declared its ideological and political attachments and relentlessly castigated progressives and liberals for reforming
the American state without fundamentally altering it. In
the radical revisionist view, the progressive-liberal tradition itself was defective.

In the field of American educational historiography,
similar critiques emerged. One aimed at shaking off the
constraints of past historical interpretations and widening
the scope of the field; the other was a radical critique of
both public schooling and the liberal tradition.

The first of these reinterpretations dates from 1960,
when Bernard Bailyn criticized the inadequacies of the
dominant tradition in educational historiography. In
Education and the Forming of American Society, Bailyn
contended that educational history-writing, for the previous six decades, had been dominated by boosters who
were primarily interested in glorifying the new profession
of education. He picked the year 1900 as the turning point,
a year when two very different histories were published,
either of which, he believed, might have served as a model
for future historians. One, Edward Eggleston's *Transit of
Civilization,* was an imaginative attempt to probe the complex roots of American culture and to analyze the traditions and ideas of the seventeenth-century colonists, the
intellectual and cultural baggage that they brought to the
new world. Bailyn thought that its major theme—the
transmission of a civilization—should have made it a

seminal work. But instead, the seminal work of the time was Thomas Davidson's *A History of Education*, which took as its theme the evolution of formal education through the ages and identified it as the best and highest form of man's endeavor. Davidson, with rhetorical gusto, maintained that "When [education] is recognized to be the highest phase of the world-process, and the teacher to be the chief agent in that process . . . then teaching is seen to be the noblest of professions, and that which ought to call for the highest devotion and enthusiasm." This zealous commitment, while appropriate for a school administrator, was inappropriate for a historian.[2]

It was obvious, Bailyn observed, why the champions of the newly emerging profession of education were taken with the Davidson view. Davidson provided them with the kind of faith and world-view that motivates crusaders. The new profession had a righteous cause, and the cause was simply that the work of the public schools was the finest achievement of American society. Once the public understood this, once the profession itself was fully developed, then no more would schoolmen be despised, and no more denied the status and income that their important work deserved.

This special sense of professional purpose, wrote Bailyn, suffused the conventional early-twentieth century works of educational history, such as Ellwood Cubberley's *Public Education in the United States* (1919) and Paul Monroe's *Textbook in the History of Education* (1906). Cubberley was an educational administrator, at one time superintendent of schools in San Francisco, who came late to historiography; Monroe taught history of education at Teachers College for twenty years and from his seminar emerged numerous histories which reflected his interpretation of American educational history. The Cubberley-Monroe thesis, put simply, held that the story of American education was the story of the emergence and triumph of the American public school; typical historical treatments scoured the past to find "seeds" of the public school, traced its evolution as an institution, described its victories over "bigots" and "reactionaries," and climaxed with its establishment as a fully realized agency of progress and good government. In this perspective, nonpublic schools were impediments, not contributors, to the democratic potential of American society.

Bailyn characterized this body of work as "the patristic literature of a powerful academic ecclesia," written "in almost total isolation from the major influences and shaping minds of twentieth-century historiography." He described their authors as "educational missionaries" who, seeking to dignify their profession, had "directed their attention almost exclusively to the part of the educational process carried on in formal institutions of instruction." By perceiving education so narrowly, "they lost the capacity to assess the variety and magnitude of the burdens it had borne and to judge its historical importance." Urging other historians "to see education in its elaborate, intricate involvement with the rest of society," Bailyn looked forward to a new historiography that would investigate the significance of family, church, community, the economy, and any other topics that might contribute to a richer understanding of "the process and content of cultural transfer."[3]

Five years after the appearance of Bailyn's essay, Lawrence A. Cremin furthered this revision of the traditional historiography in his book *The Wonderful World of Ellwood Patterson Cubberley*. Correcting Bailyn, Cremin showed that the narrowly institutional, house-history tradition which Bailyn attacked was already well established by 1900, the year Bailyn called "the turning point" in educational historiography. Cubberley's *Public Education in the United States* (1919) was of particular importance, in Cremin's view, both because "it gave a generation of American schoolmen their way of looking at the world," and because it was a "reservoir, into which flowed the principal streams of nineteenth-century thought about the development of American education."[4]

In part, the institutional, inspirational tradition could be traced to the evangelistic rhetoric of the common school reformers of the 1840s and 1850s, who saw the American common school as the finest expression of a democratic society and held closely to the New England model. Then there was the influence of the encyclopedic *American Journal of Education*, edited by school reformer Henry Barnard, himself a believer in the inspirational value of history. But most especially, there was the impact of the nation's Centennial celebration of 1876, when the United States Commissioner of Education encouraged every state and territory to prepare an educational history incorporating three points: the precursors of the public school, the origin of the public school, and the development of the public school. This national effort, which both reflected and affected public opinion, "forced the vastly different histories of the several states into a common mold and enabled them for the first time to tell a common story."[5]

During the quarter century after the Centennial, a number of state histories of education appeared, echoing what had become a consensus on the special role of the public school in American society. Works such as James Pyle Wickersham's *A History of Education in Pennsylvania* (1886) and George H. Martin's *The Evolution of the Massachusetts Public School System* (1894), both written by professional pedagogues, reiterated the increasingly familiar tale of the rise, vicissitudes, and ultimate success of the American public school. What Cremin called "the orthodox format of 1876" found repeated expression in educational histories, whether written by amateurs or by university-trained historians.[6]

Cubberley's *Public Education in the United States* was a synthesis of the conventional wisdom of at least the previous half century. It became standard fare in professional schools of education and for decades was widely considered the most authoritative text on the history of American education. Cubberley, writing in the first quarter of the twentieth century with the patriotic fervor of his time, depicted the emergence of the American public school as the capstone of a long series of struggles between the forces of progress and the forces of reaction. At every critical juncture, in Cubberley's version, the public school triumphed over the bigots and penny-pinching conservatives who tried to impede its progress.

Cremin agreed with Bailyn that Cubberley's interpretation was deeply flawed: first, by anachronism—he searched the past for the seeds of the modern public school and discarded those parts of the past that did not serve his purpose; second, by parochialism—he confused schooling with education and ignored the importance of other agencies of education, like the family and the church; and third, by evangelism—he used history as a morality tale to inspire zeal in the ranks of his profession rather than trying to understand the past on its own terms. As early as 1952, Cremin had recognized that the Cubberleyan version of history was an optimistically distorted portrait "of educational struggles which had been waged and won, and enemies which had been routed and destroyed." One consequence of this smug perspective, Cremin argued in his critique of Cubberley, was that "by portraying the great battles as over and won, it had helped to produce a generation of schoolmen unable to comprehend—much less contend with—the great educational controversies following World War II." The Cubberleyan tradition, he concluded, was "narrowly institutional, full of anachronisms, and painfully moralistic."[7]

But what was to be done to avoid the errors of the past? In Bailyn's view, the new history would have to consider education "not only as formal pedagogy but as the entire process by which a culture transmits itself across the generations. . . ." Cremin, probing "the nature and uses of education during different periods of American history," looked beyond formal schools to ask "what agencies, formal and informal, have shaped American thought, character, and sensibility over the years and what have been the relationships between these agencies and the society that has sustained them." Among these agencies he included families, churches, libraries, plantations, lyceums, museums, benevolent societies, youth groups, and military organizations. In 1970, Cremin addressed these issues in *American Education: The Colonial Experience, 1607–1783*, the first of a projected three-volume history. The book is a complex intellectual and social history of the colonial period which examines the transit of ideas and culture to the New World, demography and family, the rise of the popular press, the role of church and community, the transactions between different cultures, the ways in which diverse individuals were educated by a host of institutions, and the interrelationships among an array of converging institutions.[8]

The Bailyn-Cremin critique proved to be liberating and fruitful. It broke down the artificial barriers that had isolated educational history from the mainstream of American history; it suggested the application of social science to historical inquiry; and it widened the vision of educational historians to include the perspectives of social history, political history, intellectual history, urban history, religious history, and the history of science and technology. Still, despite the generally beneficent results of casting off the constraints of the traditional school-bound historiography, the Bailyn-Cremin revisionists have had their critics. R. Freeman Butts has rebuked the adherents of this view as "culturists" who have erred by underestimating the significance of the public school in American history; the "culturists," Butts argues, write cultural history, the effect of which is to reduce the schools to a minor role and to misunderstand their importance in helping to build an American political community.[9]

One problem of "culturist" revisionism is that, unless it is skillfully and precisely executed, educational history becomes so broad and vague that it not only merges with other disciplines, it disappears altogether. If almost everything educates, then almost every history is in some sense an educational history. Cremin has avoided this snare of vacuousness by stressing intentionality in his definition of education (he defines education as "the deliberate, systematic, and sustained effort to transmit, evoke, or acquire knowledge, attitudes, values, skills, or sensibilities, as well as any outcomes of that effort"). Nonetheless, the snare remains, in the wake of the movement away from the old constraints, away from problems with clearly defined parameters.[10]

The reaction against the Cubberley tradition has created another sort of problem for historians by seeming to belittle institutional history. It would appear that the historian who wants to study "only" schools and colleges must apologize for being narrowly institution-bound and possibly anachronistic. Yet surely the purpose of the Bailyn-Cremin critique was not to impose a new, anti-institutional orthodoxy, thus making it impossible to write about schools, but rather to stimulate both a reexamination of the assumptions that historians bring to institutions and a sensitivity to the context—political, social, and economic —within which institutions operate.

What was artificial about the Cubberleyan history was not that it was only about schools and colleges, but that it concentrated unduly on formal educational arrangements (which, of course, are most easily accessible to the historian) —laws, statements of purpose, official policies, the organization and administration of institutions—as if these were the essence of education, without according at least equal importance to how people were educated, what kinds of practices were utilized, what impact educational agencies had, how education related to broad social and political currents, and how changes came about.

The second revisionist thrust in educational historiography, which comes from a radical perspective, began in

1968 with the publication of Michael B. Katz's *The Irony of Early School Reform: Educational Innovation in Mid-Nineteenth Century Massachusetts* and continued with the appearance of books by authors such as Clarence Karier, Joel Spring, Colin Greer, Samuel Bowles, Herbert Gintis, and Walter Feinberg. The radical revisionists of educational history have attempted to repudiate liberal ideas and policies, particularly with respect to public schooling.[11]

Where liberals had argued that the spread of public schooling was social progress, radicals saw the public school as a weapon of social control and indoctrination; where liberals had maintained that reforms like compulsory schooling freed children from oppressive workplaces, radicals saw compulsory schooling as an expansion of the coercive power of the state; where liberals believed in the power of schooling to liberate people from their social origins, the radicals perceived the school as a social sorting device which undergirds an unjust, exploitative class system; where liberals considered the school to be an integral part of democratic society, radicals viewed it as a mechanism by which one group (an elite) exploits and manipulates another (the masses or the workers or the minorities or "the community"); where liberals had worked to insure that individual merit would be rewarded without regard to race or religion or other ascriptive factors, radicals described the outcome of this effort as meritocracy, hierarchy, and bureaucracy.

Interestingly, there are convergences between the two revisionist trends of the 1960s, particularly since both radicals and nonradicals seek to break free of the constraints of past tradition. Both have employed social science concepts and have turned to new data sources, such as census records, diaries, voting lists, and tax rolls. Radicals and nonradicals alike have rightly emphasized the need to study systematically both policies and practices and to investigate educational agencies not just in terms of their ideals and rhetoric, but also in terms of their actual impact on the lives they affected. Further, the radicals have influenced nonradical historians by championing the perspective of the poor and by their sensitivity to institutional bias towards various minorities.

However, the differences between the Bailyn-Cremin revisionists and the radical revisionists are significant. The historical problems that concern them are essentially different. The nonradical revisionists have sought to look at education in a broad, latitudinarian fashion, through a wide range of interacting institutions; their rewriting of the traditional history was directed against its narrow self-absorption with the public school and most especially with its methodologically unsound portrayal of history as the public school beneficently realizing itself over time. The radical historians have sought to expose and rebut the pietistic, patriotic spirit of the older historiography, but in doing so they are at least as absorbed in institutional history as the older historians and just as likely to view history as a morality tale, which, from the radical perspective, reveals the baleful influence of the public school realizing itself over time. But what most fundamentally divides the radical revisionists from others in their field is the radicals' intense and distinct ideology and politics. The work of the radical revisionists is characterized by their thorough rejection of liberal values and liberal society and their shared belief that schools were *consciously* designed by liberal reformers as undemocratic instruments of manipulation and social control. The radical indictment, in sum, is that American schools have been oppressive, not liberating, and that they were *intended* to be oppressive by those liberal reformers who developed them.

CHAPTER THREE

The Radical Perspective

THE major proponents of radical revisionism that I have singled out for particular attention in this book are in many respects a diverse group. Some are serious scholars while others are shrill polemicists. Their political orientation ranges from Marxist to anarchist, certainly a broad spectrum in terms of programmatic beliefs. Not all are historians by training; two are economists and one is a philosopher of education. There is disagreement in their work on particular issues and individuals. They approach the history of education with different styles and different individual concerns. But their diversity, real though it is, is not so great as their shared outlook. They argue that the overall direction of American history has _not_ been towards a more just society. They belittle the meliorism of reformers as inadequate or even malevolent and depict the school as an institution that coerces rather than educates.

Their works reflect the spirit of the unusual period in which they were written. Recall that the 1960s opened on a note of exuberance, in contrast to the torpor of the Eisenhower years. During the brief Kennedy administration, a liberal agenda for social reform began to take shape. In the first two years of Lyndon Johnson's tenure, this liberal agenda, now much expanded beyond the Kennedy days, was enacted, with vast sums appropriated for new programs. Expectations were high as the President and his advisers spoke of an American commitment to abolish poverty and racism in the foreseeable future.

All too soon these hopes were dashed—victims of the Vietnam war, urban riots, and persistent economic inequality. The universalism of the early civil rights movement was replaced by the separatism of black nationalists; the idealistic students who worked to enroll black voters in Mississippi in 1964 gave way to the idealistic students who employed force and issued nonnegotiable demands for power. In a remarkably short time American society moved from hope to despair and from optimism to bitterness.

Revulsion toward the war and racial injustice was nowhere stronger than on college campuses, where a radical political ideology evolved, which its leaders called the "New Left." Its adherents were passionately committed to the immediate attainment of peace, justice, and equality. The New Left portrayed the American past as a history of racism and exploitation; it scorned the political process as a sham that protected vested interests. In place of the "old" politics of compromise and conciliation, the New Left favored a "new" politics of participatory democracy and confrontation tactics.

The New Left ideology was not a refinement or extension of democratic-liberal thought but a rejection of it:
participatory democracy was urged in place of representative democracy; confrontation tactics exalted ends over
means; compromise and coalition-building were ridiculed;
and violence was condoned. The British scholar, John
Vaizey, observed in retrospect that the political outlook
of the New Left

included extreme hostility towards liberalism, impatience with
older social problems, crude anti-Americanism and association with left-wing nationalism elsewhere. . . . Its latent anti-
intellectualism and willingness to contemplate violence were
reminders of what profoundly reactionary consequences such
concepts have had in the past.[1]

The focus of democratic thought in the United States
has traditionally been a commitment to the democratic
political process, a belief in the doctrine of majority rule
and minority rights. Compromise and conciliation are
vital elements in the democratic process, because they are
the means by which diverse and competing interests are
reconciled peaceably. The process works slowly and un-
evenly, and it occasionally errs; sometimes the majority is
wrong, and sometimes the necessity for conciliation defers
needed social change. The major political parties support
the process, regardless of who wins elections or legislative
votes, because it guarantees their own ability to win some
future vote and, with it, the cooperation of the loser; this
sort of cooperation works only because it is generally understood that the majority will not tyrannize the minority.

Radicals of left and right have always perceived the relative lack of conflict in American politics as evidence that

there is no real difference between parties and candidates, that the process itself is a charade which changes nothing. They do not understand that the democratic process is meant to be a mechanism for disagreeing amicably and for arriving at decisions that satisfy the majority without crushing those who differ. The values of stability and civility, on which the democratic system depends, are widely shared because most people know that they may be in the majority on some issues and in the minority on others.

A correlate of the radical left's rejection of the political system was the belief that American written history is a tissue of legends whose purpose is to justify the status quo. Thus, one could understand events only by looking beneath the surface for purposely obscured patterns, and both Freudian and Marxist analyses provided the intellectual tools for doing so. Whether the "real" reason for some event was psychological or economic, it seemed that things were never what they appeared and that the desire of the people for radical change had been ignored or frustrated. Where liberals like John Dewey had seen education as an instrument of democratic politics to the extent that it enabled people to participate in shaping the culture and direction of their society, radicals saw education as a vehicle for teaching conformity and complacency.

The intellectual, emotional, and political currents of an era of radical protest furnished the climate within which the radical revisionist books were written. None can be said to be a systematic application of New Left thinking to educational history, but all represent different manifestations of the radical perspective of their times.

The examples of radical revisionism examined here include: Michael B. Katz's *The Irony of Early School Reform: Educational Innovation in Mid-Nineteenth Century Massachusetts*; the same author's *Class, Bureaucracy, and Schools: The Illusion of Educational Change in America*; Colin Greer's *The Great School Legend*; Clarence Karier's *Shaping the American Educational State*; the volume of essays edited by Karier, Paul Violas, and Joel Spring, *Roots of Crisis*; Joel Spring's *Education and the Rise of the Corporate State*; the same author's *A Primer of Libertarian Education*; Walter Feinberg's *Reason and Rhetoric*; a collection of essays edited by Feinberg and Henry Rosemont Jr., *Work, Technology, and Education*; and Samuel Bowles and Herbert Gintis' *Schooling in Capitalist America*. These writers do not all have precisely the same ideological commitment, nor do they all agree in their sense of what is to be done. The anarchism of Spring, for instance, is diametrically opposed to the Marxism of Bowles and Gintis; furthermore, Feinberg, a philosopher, and Bowles and Gintis, both economists, sharply criticize some of the premises of the historians. But despite their substantial differences, the various authors do share the opinion that American schools have been an *intentional, purposeful* failure and an integral part of the larger failure of American society. It is furthermore explicit in all their work that those responsible for this arrangement were not conservatives but liberals, progressives, and reformers.[2]

The essential difference between liberal and radical historians of education was well stated by Marvin Lazerson. The liberals, he writes, describe educational failures as the result of errors, of good intentions gone unpredictably wrong. But the radicals believe that our educational failures are neither accidental nor mind-less, but endemic, built into the system as part of its raison d'etre. For these historians, schools in America have acted to retain the class structure by molding the less favored to the dominant social order. They are designed to repress blacks and other non-white minorities while enhancing the growth of a professional establishment. These aims, the radical critics and historians believe, have been achieved through the construction of elaborate administrative bureaucracies impervious to reform by parents and students, by the development of ostensibly sci-entific criteria for selecting out a meritocracy, and by creating an ideology of equality of opportunity that masks the public school's real functions.[3]

Several themes deriving from this perspective appear in the radical histories. First, the school was used by the rich and the middle class as an instrument to manipulate and control the poor and the working class. Second, efforts to extend schooling to greater numbers and to reform the schools were primarily middle-class morality campaigns intended to enhance the coercive power of the school and the state. Third, an essential purpose of the school was to stamp out cultural diversity and to advance homogeneity. Fourth, the idea that upward social mobility might be achieved by children of the poor through schooling was a fable. Fifth, bureaucracy was deliberately selected as the most appropriate structure for perpetuating social stratifi-cation by race, sex, and social class. Sixth, a primary func-tion of schooling was to serve the needs of capitalism by instilling appropriate work habits in future workers.

Thus, said the radicals, those liberals and progressives who tried to make the schools better were in the end only serving the interests of the status quo. And furthermore, reformers and liberal historians of education have been responsible for the American people's failure to understand the true nature and function of schools.[4]

Refusing to accept any of the usual "givens" in American life and thought, the radicals have subjected American society and its educational institutions to relentless scrutiny. The issues they raise, as well as their aspirations, are in keeping with a long tradition of radical protest in American history. Indeed, many of their concerns connect with the earlier work of George Counts and Merle Curti, as well as the larger group of socially and politically conscious educators associated with *The Social Frontier* magazine during the Depression era. However, the radical historians of the present rarely acknowledge either a connection with or a debt to the reconstructionists of the 1930s, and more often than not criticize their predecessors as having been liberals rather than radicals.[5]

These contemporary historians have asked provocative questions about the social function of the schools. Their strictures about the antiegalitarian implications of the ideology of equal opportunity, about the relationship between educational institutions and social class, and about the values implicit in any organizational structure compel the reader to reexamine his or her own premises and to reconsider long-accepted assumptions about the purposes of schooling. Ultimately, as Carl Kaestle has pointed out, the great value of the radical critique may be that "its confirmation or rebuttal forces us to look at new questions and new data." This in itself is a valuable contribution to the field. Historians can no longer glibly write of the school as the ladder to opportunity without ascertaining who went to school, how long they stayed, and whether school-

ing had any discernible impact on their future mobility.
Similarly, the radical attack on such practices as testing,
ability grouping, and vocational guidance serves to demonstrate the need for better research into the implementation
and effect of these policies. Did they make the schools
more efficient? Was efficiency a screen for social segrega-
tion? Did they promote the identification of the most able?
Is it socially good to promote the identification of the most
able? Were the schools more democratic before the introduction of such policies? Are there cities where such
policies were not adopted, and if so, what difference did
it make; and if not, why not?[6]

The radical historians maintain that they are correcting
a false notion spread by traditional or "liberal" historians,
who misled the American people into seeing the schools
in a positive light. Michael Katz writes:

Americans share a warm and comforting myth about the
origins of public education. For the most part historians have
helped to perpetuate this essentially noble story, which portrays a rational, enlightened working class, led by idealistic
and humanitarian intellectuals, triumphantly wresting public
education from a selfish, wealthy elite and from the bigoted
proponents of orthodox religion.

Colin Greer writes disparagingly of a "great school legend,"
in which "a great nation . . . became great because of its
public schools." It is a legend, he holds, created and
purveyed by historians, especially Bernard Bailyn and
Lawrence A. Cremin, whom he identifies as apologists for
the status quo. The legend, he charges, serves to hide the
failure of ethnic and racial minorities to achieve social and
economic mobility.[7]

These complaints are actually directed at the self-congratulatory, patriotic tradition associated with Ellwood P. Cubberley, the very tradition which had been discredited by Bailyn and Cremin before the first radical history appeared. The "legend" in Greer's work had been unmasked by the very men he held responsible for it. Moreover, to debate Cubberley is to risk becoming locked into his limited framework and anachronistic concerns. As Doulgas Sloan has cautioned, it would be unfortunate if historians were

simply to stand Cubberley on his head; to retain his moralistic conflict theory of educational change, merely reversing the labels of the children of light and darkness; to substitute for his presentist history, designed to strengthen the public schools, a similarly earnest reform commitment to their demolition; to abandon his faith in the progressive evolution of educational institutions for an equally metaphysical vision of their inevitable degeneration.[8]

Both Cubberley and the radical historians argue a highly partisan interpretation. Where Cubberley saw only the public school's beneficence, the latter see only its maleficence. Where Cubberley saw it as the symbol of American success, they see it as the symbol of American failure. Like Cubberley, the radicals seek the seeds of the public school in the past, but their aim is to account for the evil that they perceive in the present. They too have a "moralistic conflict theory of educational change," but the antagonists, in their version of this conflict, are manipulative reformers on the one side and the oppressed poor on the other. But to disprove Cubberley is not to prove his opposite. The proliferation of historical research into education in the past 15 years has established, above all, how numerous are the problems that have not yet been adequately investigated and how elusive is historical certainty.

There are three analytical devices frequently encountered in the radical revisionist works. One is a sort of social and economic determinism, in which conclusions about people, events, and institutions are attributed to the assumed imperatives of social class. While Bowles and Gintis, who are Marxists, are the only authors with a clear-cut class analysis, the others persistently use the concept of social class in a deterministic manner. The second device relies on the assumption that there is a one-to-one correspondence between the ultimate effect of a policy and the intentions of its creators. The third is an institutional analysis, articulated by Michael Katz, in which it is suggested that the structure of an institution determines its purposes.

Social class analysis can be a useful tool, particularly when it sets individuals within a known world and helps to identify their associations, their personal history, and their field of action. Knowing who a person is—his assumptions, his fears, and his hopes—is important, though the historian must take care not to assume that all persons in the same socioeconomic class have identical values, hopes, and fears. The assumption that social origins are a sufficient explanation for a person's actions can lead to fallacious reductionism about causes and effects and can become a substitute for rigorous investigation of the complex political and societal sources of change.

The historian must be constantly mindful of the diversity within social and economic groupings. One need not study history to realize that businessmen are not all on the same side of every political issue, nor are all trade unionists or college professors. People with precisely the same economic self-interest often perceive it in different ways and act on it in different ways.

Social class analysis, when loosely applied, is sometimes simply vacuous generalization that explains very little. John E. Talbott points out that

it has been a common practice . . . to attach a class label to an educational institution, which is then held to respond to "needs" or "demands" of a particular social class. Who determines these needs, or whether, if such needs exist, the institution in fact responds to them, is left unclear. Moreover, such static descriptive statements, based on implicit assumptions about how the class system works, explain very little about the dynamics of the interaction between education and the structure of society. Nor do they allow for the possibility that cultural values and styles of education once presumably moored to a particular social class may drift loose from that class and become the common property of an entire society—in which case they are not particularly amenable to class analysis except in its crudest form. It is hard to see how describing an American university education as "middle class" explains very much about either the American university or American society. To be sure, education and social class have been and continue to be intimately connected. But the complexity of the historical connections between them has only begun to receive the carefully nuanced analysis it requires.[9]

But instead of carefully nuanced analysis of the connections between education and social class, the radical historians adhere to a crude sort of social and economic determinism, in which those who sought stability, order, and social harmony instead of class conflict are portrayed as allies of the elite class. This is the basis on which Clarence Karier criticizes John Dewey, and on which Paul Violas criticizes Jane Addams. Karier argues that the "mission" of the common school was to implant values "to prevent political, social, or economic revolution," and in nearly identical words, Colin Greer contends that "the common school's mission was to maintain and transmit the values considered necessary to prevent political, social, or economic upheaval." In this perspective, the historian George Counts was a good radical so long as he employed a sort of class analysis in his writings, but degenerated into a compromised liberal reformer when he fought communist infiltration of the labor movement in the mid-1930s, and, perhaps influenced by world events, shifted to a pluralist interpretation of American politics and society.[10]

Class analysis in an American context must always be carefully qualified because of the assumptions on which this kind of analysis is usually based: first, that the United States is composed of distinct and fairly rigid classes; second, that people identify themselves as members of these distinct classes; and third, that people invariably recognize and act consistently with respect to their economic self-interest. If these assumptions were valid, then one could speak authoritatively of the motives and actions of individuals and groups and arrive at historically useful judgments. But there is strong empirical evidence that class analysis is not always appropriate to the American scene because of the overlapping and crosscutting among groups and classes. Contemporary sociologists have found that the overwhelming majority of Americans, regardless of their economic position, think of themselves as middle class. In a society that lacks a widespread class consciousness and feeling of class antagonism, class analysis is of limited value. When applied rigorously, it may add some explanatory power to historical interpretation, but the historian must take care not to stress a single dimension of human motivation to the exclusion of all others.[11]

The second analytical device is a type of sociological functionalism in which inferences are loosely made about people's motives or about the hidden purposes of schools or society. The radical historian describes the terrible way things turned out and asserts that it must have been intended by policymakers. Even a century later, the eventual outcome of a policy supposedly reveals the character flaws or class prejudices of the policymakers. If a nineteenth-century reformer expressed the hope that a proposed school would diminish crime or class hostility, then this statement can be taken as "evidence" that the reformer was not really interested in promoting equality or individual mobility, even though he may have proclaimed those concerns on other occasions; furthermore, the historian infers from such statements that the "function" of the school matched the sponsor's proclaimed purpose and therefore could not have promoted equality or individual mobility. This is a self-reversing and closed argument: Bad intentions lead to bad outcomes, and bad outcomes reveal bad intentions. Because of these assumptions, it becomes unnecessary to demonstrate the link between intentions and outcomes. In one instance, a radical historian claims that "big business" and liberals brought about the Brown decision of 1954, not because of any humanitarian motives, but in order to bring blacks into the economy as skilled laborers and consumers. The "proof" is several quotes in which some businessmen and some liberals maintain that discrimination hurts the American economy; it is not clear why those statements are more meaningful than humanitarian statements made at the same time nor why anyone would believe that *any* such statements were primary explanations of complex events. The problem with such vaulting inferences is that they can neither be proved nor disproved, merely asserted. This technique of arguing about people's hidden motives—or more fallacious yet, the hidden motives of American society—fails to recognize that the consequences of a particular action cannot always be entirely controlled or fully anticipated. Rush Welter criticizes this line of analysis because

on the one hand, this approach leads to the reiterated implication that individual reformers must have sensed that the positions they adopted would serve the interests of the possessing classes. On the other, it presupposes that every individual's activity, no matter what the attitude he took toward educational issues, was part of a larger scheme of oppression and repression geared to the needs of American capitalism. From this point of view, the hopes American educators expressed for improving educational opportunity and disseminating scientific knowledge in a technological age may automatically be perceived as part of a systematic effort to seduce the working class by making them content with their place in the social hierarchy.[12]

Conjecture about reformers' motives shifts the burden of proof to the content of reformers' tracts and school officials' speeches. These are far more easily obtained and analyzed than data about the actual effects of a particular policy. The difficulty is that reformers' statements of purpose are sometimes conflicting, incomplete, inadequately formulated, or unduly optimistic. Sometimes public persons, over a long span of activity, contradict themselves or change their minds or make mistakes or overstate their case; that is why context is so important in historical research. Even when the historian knows precisely what a particular reformer said and what he meant, measuring the effect of the reformer's views on the institution he helped create is extremely problematic. A decent respect for the complexity of causation will make the historian reluctant to claim that the activities of an institution in the mid-twentieth century were directly determined by the ideas of a man who was influential in 1850.

Let us take vocational education as an example. Far more is known about the stated intentions of its proponents than about its implementation and effects. Some of its sponsors had a low regard for the intelligence and educability of immigrant children and saw vocationalism as appropriate to the immigrants' limited life opportunities; but other sponsors proposed vocational education with the expectation that it would expand opportunity for those children forced to choose between failure in the regular curriculum and dropping out to work as unskilled laborers.

We do not know to what extent vocational education matched the intention of one or the other of its advocates. We do not know enough about what would have happened to the children affected if the vocational program did not exist. We do not know how those children and their parents felt about vocationalism, whether or not they consciously chose it, or to what extent their choice was directed by school personnel. We need to know more about what happened to vocational students after they left school, what kinds of jobs they got, whether they were trapped in low-level occupations, and whether they achieved more or less mobility than similar children with different school experiences. We need studies of cities that did not offer vocational education, as well as cross-cultural research to determine how similar problems were dealt with in other nations, particularly those with different political and economic structures.[13]

A third interpretive device employed in some of the radical works is based on deductions about the relationship between the structure and the purpose of institutions. Analysis of structure is important, especially to those who study the history of schooling, but the historian must avoid the temptation to reduce the complex functioning of a major social institution to simple and deterministic generalizations. The same structure may perform differently at different times, depending on the historical situation. It is necessary to reconstruct particular institutions within the context of their time and to assess the interaction among structure, function, and purpose with the awareness that individuals within given institutions often use them to achieve their own goals regardless of the apparent dictates of structure.

This approach is most often used by radical historians in arguing that bureaucracy was purposely chosen to institutionalize racism and social class bias in the schools. "Forms of organizational structure are not and cannot be neutral," contends Michael Katz. "The relationships between bureaucracy, class bias, and racism are fixed." The emergence of bureaucracy as the dominant organizational form of public education was neither a historical accident nor an inevitable process, he maintains, but a congruence of purpose and structure: "There is a functional relationship between the way in which schools are organized and what they are supposed to do." American education for the past century has been "universal, tax-supported, free, compulsory, bureaucratic, racist, and class-biased." It might have been different, he believes, if some other form of organization had been chosen:

In fact, on closer inspection, it appears that bureaucracy is inevitable only when men confront certain problems with particular social values and priorities. It is not industrialization that makes bureaucracy inevitable, but the combination of industrialization and particular values. . . . Bureaucracy came about because men confronted particular kinds of social problems with particular social purposes. Those purposes reflected class attitudes and class interests. Modern bureaucracy is a bourgeois invention; it represents a crystallization of bourgeois social attitudes.[14]

Katz contends that other, more humane alternatives were available but were ignored or rejected by school reformers since bureaucracy fit their purpose of disciplining children for the industrial order. What were these alternatives? Katz identifies them as "paternalistic voluntarism," "democratic localism," and "corporate voluntarism." The paradigm of "paternalistic voluntarism" was the New York Public School Society, whose self-perpetuating board of trustees sponsored free schooling during the first half of the nineteenth century. As Katz notes, the schools of the Society represented "a class system of education . . . a vehicle for the efforts of one class to civilize another." But the paternalistic voluntarism of the New York Public School Society was not an alternative to bureaucracy; in fact, as Carl Kaestle documents, the New York Public School Society "displayed incipient bureaucracy from the start," and by mid-century "nearly all of the features associated with modern urban school bureaucracies were already evident" in its schools.[15]

Katz's second alternative, "democratic localism," was embodied in the small, locally controlled school district. His first example is an 1841 plan to divide New York City into independent school districts, which was advocated at the time as an alternative to the bureaucratic control of Katz's first model, the New York Public School Society. Katz does not mention that democratic localism was adopted in New York City in 1842 and that it quickly sprouted into localized bureaucracies.[16]

Katz's third alternative to bureaucracy is "corporate voluntarism," which was typified by the organization of independent academies and colleges ("individual corporations operated by self-perpetuating boards of trustees and financed either wholly through endowment or through a combination of endowment and tuition"). Though Katz does not dwell on the question of whom these privately endowed, tuition-charging academies and colleges served and whom they excluded, there can be little doubt that corporate voluntarism represented another version of class education—the provision of advanced education by the well-to-do for their own children. Over time, corporate voluntarism evolved the bureaucratic features that are now found in most universities, resulting not from personal whim or class conspiracy but from diverse pressures for fair and uniform treatment of faculty and students.[17]

In sum, Katz's three alternatives are no alternatives at all, for all of them either were bureaucratic at the outset or became bureaucratic. Similarly, Katz's assertion that bureaucracy is a "crystallization of bourgeois social values" fails to account for the appearance of bureaucracy in non-bourgeois societies. The fact that bureaucracy is a characteristic organizational form in socialist and communist nations indicates that it is not a "bourgeois invention" but a complex response to population growth, urbanization, and modernization. While there is abundant historical evidence that cultural chauvinists in the United States wanted only to assimilate newcomers completely into their own culture, it is unclear just how integral the bureaucratic revolution was to this goal; bureaucratic school systems were also created by some minorities (notably, Catholics) and emerged in culturally homogeneous areas as well.

This blending of class analysis and institutional analysis in Katz's work is supposed to show how class motives dictated certain institutional arrangements. But delving into the motives of those who founded bureaucratic institutions, while it may be significant for social and intellectual historians, is no substitute for careful investigation of the objective conditions that prompted school reformers to look for different ways to organize schools. Nor can it explain the large historical forces at work in different cities, different cultures, and different nations.

While it is interesting to know the stated motives of reformers and the rationale for formal bureaucratic structures, such concerns are a starting point for analysis, not the analysis itself. As previously noted, it is far easier for a historian to document the stated intentions of reformers and to delineate administrative arrangements than it is to discover how a complex institution actually worked and what it meant to the people affected by it. The British historian Harold Silver has argued that this focus on "the structure of educational systems, the motives of providers, [and] the intricacies of policies" has been responsible for neglect of far more important aspects of the history of education and schooling and has contributed to "widespread historical ignorance, 'disguised' . . . by the very bulk of what has been written." When Silver researched the history of a monitorial school for the poor in early nine-teenth-century London, he found little in contemporary scholarship to explain what he encountered. Historians of nineteenth-century education have presented the monitorial system, Silver notes, as "a wraith," and their histories are replete with "abundant statements about the intentions of the founders of the monitorial system, about its stated methods, about its defects, its critics and its demise—but nothing about the detailed operation of monitorial schools, no attempts to match theory with reality." Somewhat to his surprise, then, Silver learned that the particular school he selected had

a more imaginative and humane approach to children and to school affairs, and stronger school-community links than we had expected, or could explain. The school was as concerned in its early decades with the children's health as it was with their souls, and the school and its managers were the focal point for Lambeth's fight against cholera, bad sanitation and other environmental nuisances. The teachers were competent and the school efficient. From the 1880s boys were winning a stream of scholarships to London's grammar and other schools. A record of humanity, efficiency and—in a variety of ways—innovation seemed to stretch from the 1820s to the twentieth century.

Yet most of what had been written about popular school-ing in this period "offered few or no real clues as to rela-tionships in schools, their role in the community, or as to the social structures and processes, controversies and chang-ing ideas and assumptions, in which education was in-tricately involved." Silver discovered that knowing the intentions of the school's founders, its organizational chart, and its formal policies was not the same as understanding the impact of the school on the community, the way it was used by its students, and the quality of educational experience that it offered.[18]

Another example of misplaced emphasis on the inter-relationship between social class and bureaucratic structure is David C. Hammack's interpretation of the centralization and professionalization of New York City's public school system. Hammack's analysis of what happened and why is narrowly tuned to the social class identity of the centralizers, many of whom were listed in the Social Register. The study minimizes the sorry state of the schools before centralization—the overcrowding, the physical deterioration of buildings, the lockstep instruction, the favoritism in hiring, and the iron grip of a meritless seniority system. By concentrating on the reformers' social origins, the author overlooks the ironic fact that an inflexible bureaucracy had already grown up in the city's schools while they were controlled by powerful local boards, many of which were dominated by ethnic minorities. Also slighted is the interesting process by which an elite managed to convince a popularly elected mayor and state legislature to approve centralization, as well as the way in which the centralized system was taken over by the middle class and the lower-middle class when the elite reformers lost political power. No one in the Social Register became a supervisor or teacher in the newly centralized system; the central board had a reform majority for less than three years and was subsequently controlled by Tammany appointees. Instead of giving power over minorities to upper-class nativists, as Hammack implies, centralization may actually have hastened the dominance of Irish Catholics in the New York City public schools.[19]

Another consideration is the possibility that, given the nature of schools *at that time*, administrative reforms may have been appropriate. In New York City, the centralized system fostered educational innovation in ways that the decentralized boards had never done. For the first time, school officials created programs to serve the entire community, not just those children who signed up before registration closed. Consider the following programs initiated after centralization: classes for the physically handicapped, blind, deaf, tubercular, and anemic; evening recreation centers for teenagers; evening concerts, vacation schools, and playgrounds; medical inspections; high schools; special classes for non-English-speaking children and adults; evening lectures for adults; school libraries. School officials wanted every child to be in some kind of school. Radical historians such as Joel Spring and Colin Greer would say of the centralizers that they merely wanted to enhance their own power and extend their control over the city's children. But one cannot avoid the suspicion that in bringing this kind of indictment against school centralization, such critics are projecting their own values and the perceptions of their own time in an inappropriate way. For one thing, the innovations introduced by the centralizers were popular: millions of people annually attended the lectures, concerts, and recreation centers, voluntarily; and, for the first time, provision was made for children who had previously been neglected or excluded because of their handicaps.[20]

But were these improvements merely window dressing for the sinister goings-on in the classrooms? It is not clear that school life was perceived to be as repressive to children and parents of seventy-five years ago as it now seems to have been to some contemporary eyes. Indeed, turn-of-the-century Jewish parents on the lower East Side nearly rioted when their children were not admitted to public schools because of overcrowding. It was then the practice of school officials to turn children away once the school register was filled, and each year thousands of children were refused admission. Jewish immigrant parents and their children, newly arrived from countries where exclusion of Jews from state schools was a common practice, fairly besieged the public schools, as well as vacation schools, night schools, and libraries. A government report in 1900 noted with some amazement that "the poorest among them will make all possible sacrifices to keep his children in school. . . ." Yet these public schools into which Jews demanded admission and for which they made sacrifices were even then deplored by school reformers as physically decrepit and educationally backward. From the perspective of the radical historians, who see the school as an institution fastened on the immigrants by those who wished to control them, the Jewish demand for public schooling is inexplicable.[21]

Nor does the radical perspective explain the angry response of poor immigrant parents in New York City in 1917, who defeated a mayor for trying to introduce progressive educational reforms into *their* schools. The reform proposal, known as the Gary plan for the town in Indiana where it originated, was then in the mainstream of progressive education as a means of combining work, study, and play and making the schools more like "real" life. While there was a great deal to be said for the Gary plan, many poor parents feared that its real intent was to con-

vert the curriculum to an emphasis on industrial education and to deny their children a traditional education
and the chance to improve themselves through schooling.
Proponents of the plan couldn't understand the opposition; they thought that the Gary plan would be more
popular, more efficient, and more economical than existing schools, but they miscalculated popular sentiment
about the schools. The particulars of the controversy are
not nearly so significant in this context as the fact that
immigrant parents defended the traditional public school
and displayed a proprietary sense about an institution
from which, according to today's radical historians, they
were supposed to be alienated.[22]

A nonradical account of the bureaucratic revolution is
found in Selwyn K. Troen's study of the St. Louis public
schools. Troen specifically rejects the idea that bureaucratic
reforms were an upper-class power strategy, because "it is
mere inference to assert that the presence of social-register
types on the board represents a concerted attempt at social
control." Why did St. Louis, like other major American
cities, turn to the bureaucratic factory model for its
schools? Troen answers, "It was born of necessity as educators first confronted the problems of managing a rapidly
expanding and increasingly complex institution." Furthermore, he found that bureaucratization removed the schools
from rancorous, divisive politics and that this change won
public approval.

In the space of only a generation, public education had left
behind a highly regimented and politicized system dedicated
to training children in the basic skills of literacy and the special
discipline required of urban citizens, and had replaced it with
a largely apolitical, more highly organized and efficient struc-

ture specifically designed to teach students the many specialized skills demanded in a modern, industrial society. In terms of programs this entailed the introduction of vocational instruction, a doubling of the period of schooling, and a broader concern for the welfare of urban youth.

The reformed, bureaucratized system was "shaped by the society it was designed to serve." According to Troen, it served the city's needs at that time, and St. Louisans trusted the system.[23]

Troen tries to understand the issues as they were understood at the time. He does not compromise his own sensibility, nor does he chide people of another era for lacking his values and knowledge. His work stands in contrast to that of radical historians, who offer moralistic condemnation instead of understanding, and hindsight instead of insight. The historian is privileged to know not only how things were eventually to turn out but also the impact on his subject of large social and economic changes elsewhere in the society. It is easy, with hindsight, to recognize error and shortsightedness. It is more difficult, but no less significant, to document how and why people made certain choices, not only in terms of the limitations imposed by their values and perceptions, but also in terms of the influence of historic forces that they could neither foresee nor control.

CHAPTER FOUR

Coercive Education: The Radical View

A MAJOR radical leitmotif is the charge that the public school was an instrument of coercive assimilation, designed to strip minority children of their culture and to mold them to serve the needs of capitalism. Michael Katz initiated this discussion with the charge that educational reform was imposed by social leaders on "an often skeptical, sometimes hostile, and usually uncomprehending working class," and that it was characterized by "the mentality of cultural absolutism." He contends in *Class, Bureaucracy, and Schools* that the public schools were organized and structured specifically to reinforce the bias of the larger society and to secure cultural homogeneity. Clarence Karier claims that liberal reformers shaped the public schools as "a vehicle of social control and order," which was used by the state for "cultural indoctrination," thus adjusting diverse minorities to their place in the social order and preventing violent revolution.[1]

This view of education as a means of cultural oppression is representative of the radical contention that "education was something the better part of the community did to the others to make them orderly, moral, and tractable." The trouble with this line of analysis is that it treats both schools and minority groups in stereotypical fashion: Schools are oppressive; minority groups are oppressed. So simplistic an approach cannot provide the intellectual groundwork for serious history. Just to consider the diverse types of minorities in American history is to become aware of the wide range of problems and responses that have characterized educational efforts. There have been racial minorities, religious minorities, linguistic minorities, and national minorities. Each has had its own educational needs, which have been met or not met in different ways. It is historically unjustified to assert that all have been crushed by their education or by the public schools into a homogeneous, deracinated mass.[2]

In examining the history of various minority groups—racial, religious, linguistic, and cultural—it becomes clear that they cannot be considered simplistically or stereotypically. When each group is looked at on its own terms, several important points emerge. First, it is fallacious to lump together all minority groups as "the oppressed" or "the repressed," as though their experiences, their problems, and their attitudes were interchangeable. Second, it is untenable to assume that each minority group was monolithic; within each group, there were usually different factions and opposing views about the desirability of assimilating. Third, the way a particular group was treated differed, sometimes dramatically, from one time period to another; attitudes about assimilation and cultural diversity changed with the social climate. Fourth, not all schooling of minorities took place in public schools; the decision to respect the right of minorities to maintain private schools was itself public policy and has been repeatedly safeguarded by the Supreme Court.

During the second half of the nineteenth century, public schools were firmly established throughout the country; the New England ideology, which asserted that the survival of the American republic was dependent on the public schools, became commonplace. The ideology seems to have been more a selling point for public support than an article of faith, however. If Americans really believed that the nation's institutions and freedom depended on the strength of the common schools, they would have prohibited nonpublic education. But Americans apparently respected freedom of choice more than the common school ideology, for private schools, operated by particularistic groups, abounded. Indeed, there was remarkable diversity, both in private and public schools. In addition to schools sponsored by religious groups, private foreign language schools were established by Germans, Poles, French Canadians, Czechs, Norwegians, Dutch, Lithuanians, Jews, Japanese, Koreans, Chinese, and others. Bilingual programs could be found in many nineteenth-century private and public schools, particularly in the Midwest, where there were large islands of Germans, and in the Far West, where both California and New Mexico had Spanish bilingual schools. Baltimore and Indianapolis had public German bilingual school systems during the nineteenth century, and the public schools of Cincinnati had a fully developed German bilingual program from 1840 until 1917.[3]

While there have been bitter political struggles over the issue of subsidizing Catholic schools, the right of nonpublic schools to exist was never seriously in jeopardy until the 1920s. Inspired by the xenophobic post-World War I climate, the voters of Oregon adopted an initiative measure in 1922 which would have required parents to send their children to public schools. The purpose of the measure, aimed especially at immigrants and Catholics, was to forcibly Americanize all children by putting them into the same public classrooms. David Tyack has described how the bill's publicists, who included the Ku Klux Klan, employed a twisted version of the common school ideal to insist "that the public school should mix children of all the people—all ethnic groups, all economic classes—in order to produce social solidarity. . . ." Klan spokesmen did not recognize the irony of their advocacy of social, racial, and economic integration. The attorney for the state of Oregon used traditional egalitarian rhetoric to maintain that

the great danger overshadowing all others which confront the American people is the danger of class hatred. History will demonstrate the fact that it is the rock upon which many a republic has been broken and I don't know any better way to fortify the next generation against that insidious poison than to require that the poor and the rich, the people of all classes and distinction, and of all different religious beliefs, shall meet in the common schools, which are the great American melting pot.

Happily for the nonpublic schools of America, the United States Supreme Court in 1925 declared Oregon's law unconstitutional and held it to be an unreasonable interference with the liberty of parents to direct their children's education. The state does not have the power, wrote the Court in *Pierce v. Society of Sisters*, "to standardize its children by forcing them to accept instruction from public teachers only."[4]

During the same period, the Supreme Court was called on not only to guarantee the nonpublic schools' right to exist, but also to protect the freedom to teach foreign languages. The ugly side of the postwar Americanization crusade gave vent to intense anti-German feelings, which led most states to adopt laws restricting foreign language instruction in both public and nonpublic schools. Many states required English as the basic language of instruction (there had been foreign language schools where English was rarely spoken). Some states, like Nebraska, went further; in 1919, it prohibited the teaching of any modern language in the first eight grades of all public and nonpublic schools. When a parochial school teacher in Nebraska was convicted of teaching German, he carried his appeal to the Supreme Court. In *Meyer v. Nebraska* (1923), without questioning the state's power to require English instruction, the Supreme Court overturned Nebraska's law and reaffirmed the teacher's right to teach and the parent's right to engage a teacher without state interference. Similarly, when Americanizers passed a law in Hawaii to force the use of English as the exclusive language of instruction in Japanese private schools, the Japanese went to court and won.[5]

Where educational oppression of a minority was blatant

and purposeful, as in the case of the American Indian, the policy was a disaster which neither educated nor assimilated. Through most of American history, missionaries and government officials took it as their duty to civilize and Christianize the Indians; usually this meant that Indian culture and language and folkways had to be eliminated. While some were "weaned away from the blanket," as the saying went, most simply developed a strong internal resistance to the new behavior. Forced efforts at assimilation tended to produce precisely the opposite of what was intended.

Before the Civil War, most missionary schools favored bilingual instruction using Indian languages. Additionally, there were many Indian-initiated schools. The Cherokees, in particular, had created their own school system, which sent graduates to Eastern colleges; further, they published a bilingual newspaper using a Cherokee alphabet devised by a member of the tribe in 1821. Schools were also run by Choctaws, Creeks, and Seminoles. However, in the 1870s, while a number of tribes were making their last stands in battle, the federal government launched a new boarding school program designed to extirpate Indian culture. Indian children were separated from their families and reservation, forced to abandon their native language, and wholly removed from tribal lore and mores.[6]

This policy of coercive assimilation was changed during the New Deal, when efforts were made to strengthen tribal self-government and to encourage cultural freedom for Indians. For the first time, the Bureau of Indian Affairs emphasized bilingualism, native teachers, adult education, and preservation of the Indians' cultural heritage. By 1943, most federal schools were day schools, not boarding schools. Though there was a reversion to the rapid assimilationist approach in the 1950s at the height of superpatriotic fervor, these policies were repudiated in the 1960s when the federal government took decisive steps to transfer control of Indian schools to Indians.

The story of Indian education in the United States illustrates the variability of the historical experience— even when it is that of a clearly oppressed group. It is a history that most nearly fits the radical concept of schooling as a tool of coercion and imposition. And yet to read it only from that perspective would be to miss a number of intriguing divergences. The very substantial shift to pluralistic policies in the 1930s and then again in the 1960s underlines the struggle between opposing philosophies, rather than the predetermined, unvarying capitalistic program of oppression that the radicals describe. The existence of Indian schools in the nineteenth century suggests that Indians themselves were not necessarily hostile to schooling but to cultural suppression. It further suggests that a policy of cultural respect, in this as in other instances, would have stimulated Indian educational efforts and, ultimately, Indian assimilation on terms set by Indians.

The case of black educational history also defies the simplistic labels of ideologically determined history, but for different reasons. Whereas government policy attempted to force the assimilation and de-ethnicization of Indians, it explicitly sought to prevent the assimilation of blacks. Whereas the cultural aspirations of European immigrant groups were at least tolerated and frequently encouraged, those of blacks were ignored, or, worse, ridiculed. The doctrine of white supremacy was used to justify social and economic repression of blacks, in both North and South.

Yet black educational history is not a story of schooling imposed on unwilling black masses but rather of schooling denied to black masses. One of the most fascinating aspects of black history is the remarkable struggle of blacks, both slave and free, to obtain an education despite legal barriers. "Believing that slaves could not be enlightened without developing in them a longing for liberty," the slave states adopted laws prohibiting the education of slaves. The slaveholders could not risk permitting the spread of literacy, for once a slave learned to read there was no controlling what he might read; ignorance, not schooling, was the best form of social control. Some states expelled free Negroes because they might have access to abolitionist literature and spread the contagion of insurrection to those who were illiterate. In some parts of the Deep South, even the education of free blacks was forbidden. Yet even within the slave system there were individuals who found a way to steal the closely guarded secrets of literacy; some slaves developed personal relationships with their masters and, as favored house servants, acquired literacy; some plantations, for their own internal purposes, trained slaves as skilled craftsmen who required some ability to read. Nonetheless, the laws forbidding the education of slaves were largely effective, and not more than 1 or 2 percent of the slave population was literate.[7]

The "free persons of color," who numbered about a half-million in 1860 and were evenly divided between North and South, faced a different set of obstacles. Though the restrictions on their ability to get an education were not as onerous as those aimed at slaves, they too had to overcome tremendous odds to become literate. Schools for free blacks operated, despite white hostility, in most parts of the North and in defiance of the laws in the South. In Southern cities, legislation barring the schooling of blacks was often laxly enforced, and black schools were either tolerated or functioned clandestinely. Thomas Sowell has gathered literacy data for "free persons of color" in the antebellum era and has found that, in fifteen out of sixteen cities studied, the majority of free blacks was literate even though few blacks were officially reported as attending any school. In Savannah, where not a single black was officially in school, more than two-thirds of the free black population were literate; in Charleston, the illiteracy rate among free black adults was less than 2 percent. Southern cities, unlike plantations and rural areas, provided an atmosphere in which social control was diffuse and in which it was possible for black schools to survive despite legal prohibition.[8]

Before Emancipation, slaveowners feared that education would awaken a longing for liberty in slaves; after Emancipation, reactionary Southern whites feared that it would encourage a longing for equality. If today's radical historians were correct in their hostility to schooling, then Southern whites would have rushed to create school systems for newly freed blacks in order to control and indoctrinate them. But, to the contrary, the historical record shows that the schooling of blacks was imposed on a reluctant and hostile white South by the might of the federal government and the zeal of Northern idealists. After the war's conclusion, a network of schools run by benevolent societies, missionaries, and the Freedmen's Bureau sprang into existence, staffed mostly by Northern teachers who stressed liberal arts rather than practical education.

Many of the mission schools taught classical languages, which Southern whites thought absurd. Senator John C. Calhoun of South Carolina had once said that he would be willing to believe in the possibility of black equality if ever he met a black who could parse a Latin verb or write the Greek alphabet. This oft-quoted remark was frequently cited in the autobiographical accounts of college-educated blacks of the first free generation, and these schools, according to Horace Mann Bond, "provided for Southern Negroes some of the most effective educational institutions the world has ever known." Newly freed blacks eagerly sought the schooling that had so long been denied them, and black delegates to Reconstruction-era state constitutional conventions espoused the provision of public schooling that was compulsory and open to all.[9]

After the end of Reconstruction, when blacks lost the protection of the federal government, white Southerners took advantage of blacks' political impotence and put severe handicaps on black schools. Southern whites knew that they had to offer some schooling for blacks, but it was as minimal as could be managed, and the emphasis was on industrial rather than liberal education. The meagerness of educational arrangements for blacks was an implicit acknowledgment by the white leaders that too much schooling might be a dangerous thing and might unsettle the racial caste system. Radical historians today describe the public high school as an innovation that was imposed on a reluctant community by prestigious social leaders for selfish purposes, but in the South it was the prestigious white leaders who resisted establishing high schools for blacks. Black high schools were provided long after white high schools and then only with great reluctance and with continued stress on industrial education rather than a college curriculum. The reluctance, of course, came from whites, not blacks. By contrast, the nation's first black public high school was founded in Washington, D.C., in 1870 by blacks. The school, which was eventually known as the Dunbar High School, was a model of academic excellence which frequently out-performed all-white schools on citywide tests. Over its eighty-five-year history, more than three-quarters of Dunbar's students went on to college, and its alumni include the nation's first black general, the first black cabinet member, the first black federal judge, the discoverer of blood plasma, and the first black United States senator since Reconstruction, as well as more recipients of academic doctorates than any other black high school in the nation.[10]

The provision of schooling in the South lagged far behind the rest of the nation until the mid-twentieth century. For Southern blacks, both the quantity and quality of schooling was far below that available to Southern white students. The consequence of generations of educational deprivation is that black educational attainment has historically been far less than white educational attainment; only in the past decade has the black-white differential in years of schooling narrowed significantly. This disparity in educational attainment has contributed to social and economic inequality. The point that eludes today's radical historians is that blacks were more often oppressed by the education that they did not receive than by the education that they did receive.

If the radical description of the school as an alien institution imposed on the community by elitists does not fit black history, it is equally at variance with the experience of European immigrants. It is instructive to contrast the radicals' hostile portrait of public schools with the autobiographical account of Theodore Dreiser, who grew up in the late nineteenth century in the Midwest. The son of poor German Catholics, Dreiser hated the Catholic schools, which to him were dogmatic and terrifying, and claimed that "it was the seeds here sown that definitely alienated me from the Church." When at last his mother permitted him to go to public school, he was overjoyed:

Truly, I think my young American soul gave one bound and thereby attained to the meaning of freedom! I could almost hear the timbers of an antiquated and repressive educational system creaking and crashing about me. This girl, who was to be my teacher and who did really teach me in the best sense of the word, spelled opportunity instead of repression. . . . Whenever I think of the American school system as it was then—the genial shepherding of millions of children after the fashion of loving parents, and with more love and much more intelligence and care than most of the poorer parents have to offer—I still hold to some slight faith in, if not democracy, at least some form of social organization which would permit of the child being as advantageously and intensively cultivated as any other living and cultivable thing.[11]

There is nothing in the radical histories that prepares the reader to understand Dreiser's description of either Catholic schools or public schools.

The same reductionist approach flaws the radicals' depiction of Americanization and assimilation programs as cultural coercion imposed on hapless immigrants. To be sure, Americanization efforts frequently were crudely chauvinistic, and by present-day standards the very concept of Americanization seems to be an unwarranted intervention into people's private lives. But the process was not simply a one-way transaction between victim and oppressor. Immigrant groups were themselves sponsors of many assimilation and Americanization programs. Timothy L. Smith has documented an immigrant thirst for education which is sharply at variance with the radical image of coercion and brutalization. Smith points out that the night school movement was started by immigrant associations, then adopted by the public schools. Early parochial schools "stressed the learning of English quite as much as the preservation of Old World culture." Far from fighting to withdraw to ethnic enclaves, immigrants

realized that to learn to speak and read English was to make their investment of time, expense, and emotion gilt-edged. The earliest volumes of virtually any Slavic newspaper published by religious or secular organizations in America carried lessons in English, announced the publication of simple dictionaries or grammars, and exhorted readers to learn the new tongue as a means of getting and holding a better job.

But their self-Americanization was not necessarily at the expense of their cultural values; Slovaks, Greeks, Hungarians, Serbs, Romanians, and Russians sent their children to public schools, but also "insisted upon frequent and sometimes daily attendance at the church for catechetical instruction, precisely as Orthodox Jewish parents sent their youngsters from public schools to the synagogue in the late afternoon or on Sunday." Many immigrants had a secure sense of the value of their own heritage. Jane Addams recalled lecturing Greek immigrants on the glories of America's past; when she was done, one of her audience remarked, quietly but assuredly, that his own Greek ancestors were better than her Anglo-Saxon forebears. Even while imbibing literacy, patriotism, and the fundamentals of citizenship, immigrant minorities maintained their cultural heritage in ethnic associations, religious institutions, newspapers, and a host of other communal activities.[12]

John Walker Briggs, in his study of the Italian community in three American cities, found that the immigrants' church and the Italian press actively promoted Americanization and the value of schooling. In the same vein, Mordecai Soltes described the Yiddish press of New York City as "an Americanizing agency." At the time of World War I, there were five Yiddish-language newspapers with a circulation of half a million readers. These newspapers consistently supported the public schools as well as supplementary religious instruction. The Yiddish press, wrote Soltes, "actively cooperates with the civic and patriotic purposes of the school." To assume with the perspective of the late twentieth century that the immigrants who furthered their own Americanization had been indoctrinated is to credit them with little intelligence or self-interest. It is more likely that they took from these programs what they wanted and ignored what they did not want.[13]

Heinz Kloss, a German scholar of national minority laws, has found American policy toward its non-English-speaking minorities to be remarkably tolerant. Americans have the right to use their mother tongue at home and in public; the right to establish private cultural, economic, and social institutions in which their mother tongue is spoken; the right to cultivate their mother tongue in private schools—which are not only tolerated but granted a state charter with tax-exempt status. The cultural freedoms which are taken for granted in the United States are not matched by many other nations. Kloss does not agree with those radical historians who argue that the homogeneity of the American people is the result of persistently coercive educational efforts to strip minorities of their differences. He holds that

the non-English ethnic groups in the United States of America were Anglicized not because of nationality laws which were unfavorable towards their languages but in spite of nationality laws favorable to them. Not by legal provisions and measures of authorities, not by the state did the nationalities become assimilated, but by the absorbing power of the unusually highly developed American society. The nationalities could be given as many opportunities as possible to retain their identity, yet the achievements of the Anglo-American society and the possibilities for individual achievements and advancements which this society offered were so attractive that the descendants of the "aliens" sooner or later voluntarily integrated themselves into this society.[14]

In much the same vein, Joshua Fishman attributes the rapid absorption of non-English-speaking minorities to the openness of American society, not to educational coercion. Noting that American nationalism has always been "nonethnic" in character, Fishman writes that "there was no apparent logical opposition between the ethnicity of incoming immigrants and the ideology of America. Individually and collectively immigrants could accept the latter without consciously denying the former. However, once they accepted the goals and values of Americans, the immigrants were already on the road to accepting their lifestyles, their customs, and their language."[15]

Assimilation was facilitated, if Kloss and Fishman are correct, by *lack* of oppression. Specific instances of discrimination against foreign children have usually been traced to the attitudes of teachers, an Anglo-centric curriculum, and a generalized American disparagement of Old World cultures. More often than not, this discrimination was sporadic rather than systematic. Had it been more substantive and more threatening, it would probably have impeded assimilation by raising immigrant self-consciousness and resistance. Where educational policy was coercive, as it was towards Indians and blacks, it was least successful in promoting education, assimilation, or social harmony. It would appear that the best way to promote these ends is in an atmosphere of cultural pluralism and individual freedom.

CHAPTER FIVE

Education and Social Mobility: The Radical Case Examined

A CENTRAL motif in radical histories is the assertion that the schools did not foster social and economic mobility. In fact, some of the radicals doubt that there ever was much mobility in American society. They argue that the existence of public schools made it possible to legitimate inequality by appearing to offer equal opportunity to succeed through education. But, they contend, only those from high-status families do well in school, so the injustice of the social order is reproduced and perpetuated through the myth and mechanism of the public school.

Joel Spring holds that schooling may have *curtailed*

mobility: "It could be argued that the possibility of movement between social classes has steadily decreased in the
United States in the twentieth century with the implementation of universal schooling." Katz, on the other hand,
views the school as a ladder of mobility for the middle class
but not for the poor because schools were "designed to
reflect and confirm the social structure that created them."
Colin Greer contends that the presumed relation between
schooling and mobility is "entirely fallacious." Indeed, he
writes, "We must not only dismiss the image of rapid
mobility and assimilation, but must place, in its stead, an
image of a moderately restrictive and fundamentally segre-
gationist society." Bowles and Gintis hold that "education
over the years has never been a potent force for economic
equality." They state further that the rapid extension of
educational attainment has led neither to an increase in
economic mobility nor to a diminution of the importance
of family background on educational attainment. The
school, they find, is "but one of several institutions which
serve to perpetuate . . . economic inequality and social
immobility." Karier states that "one of the central myths
of the twentieth century is that schooling will result in
social mobility."[1]

To test these claims of social immobility and the irrelevance of schooling, it is necessary to examine both historical and contemporary evidence for answers to two
separate questions: First, has American society generally
been characterized by mobility or immobility, and second,
what influence, if any, has schooling had on mobility patterns? If the radical picture is correct, then American
society is locked into rigid class patterns which are undis-
turbed by more or less schooling. But if upward mobility

has been widespread, then the radical analysis is a misrepresentation of American history; and if schooling has facilitated upward mobility, then they have misrepresented the social function of schooling.

In recent years, there have been a number of historical studies that attempt to measure rates of social mobility in a particular place during a particular period by following the careers of a large group of individuals. At issue in such studies is whether American society has been relatively open or restricted. Merging the interests of the sociologist with those of the historian, such research is made feasible by the availability of computers and modern sampling techniques, which permit the processing of large quantities of data. Part of the appeal of this approach is that it offers a way to test reality against rhetoric (was the American promise of opportunity reality or illusion?), and it poses a means of writing about the experiences of ordinary people who left no diaries or records behind. Such research has the potential to shed new light on basic social processes and mass behavior and to reveal a dimension of historical reality that might not have been apparent, either to contemporaries or to historians consulting traditional sources.

It is possible, for example, to gain evidence from these studies about the occupational structure (was it fluid or static?), about the opportunities available to unskilled workers (were they likely to begin and end their careers in the same slot?), about the inheritance of status across generations (were workers' sons trapped in their fathers' occupations?), about the nature of poverty, about the relative importance of racial and ethnic discrimination, about differences in the experiences of various immigrant groups. These are questions important to the American experience, and the development of the technical means to ask them is a promising field for future research.

Generally, the historian preparing such a study uses the federal census either to draw a random sample (for a large city) or to trace an entire segment of the population in a smaller city. Beginning in 1850, the federal census listed individuals by name and gave their occupation, birthplace, property holdings, literacy, and other information. The federal census can be supplemented by data from the state census, tax rolls, and local directories to trace individuals from one decade to the next and discern changes in occupation, property holdings, and residence. There are problems with this technique that every historian is aware of: the language barrier between census-takers and foreigners; the fact that some people are missed, either because they moved in and out of town between censuses or because they were overlooked (and the poorest were likeliest to be "lost" by the enumerators, especially in big cities); the information given to the census-taker was not necessarily accurate; because of high rates of residential mobility, many individuals appear once and then disappear, probably having moved to another city. It may be, though it is not certain, that the least successful are likeliest to move and drop out of the historian's trace, which would skew the outcome; however, this problem is common to all mobility studies of the nineteenth century, which makes their findings roughly comparable.

A pioneer study of great influence has been Stephan Thernstrom's *Poverty and Progress: Social Mobility in a Nineteenth Century City*, which went through more than a dozen printings in the decade after its appearance in 1964. *Poverty and Progress* examines career patterns of unskilled laborers (the lowest occupational group) and their sons in Newburyport, Massachusetts, from 1850 to 1880. Thernstrom's purpose, as he states at the outset, was to test the American "myth"—the belief in America as a land of opportunity for the common man—against the "social reality" of a single nineteenth century city.[2]

Thernstrom found that one of ten unskilled laborers rose to become skilled craftsmen, and only one in twenty were able to lift themselves into nonmanual jobs. He noted too that occupational mobility rates were distinctly lower for immigrants than for native-born workers. Further, only 19 percent of the sons of laborers rose to skilled jobs and 10 percent to nonmanual jobs, while 71 percent remained in either unskilled or semiskilled occupations. The Irish were particularly successful in accumulating property even though they were unsuccessful in climbing out of low-status occupations; most Irish workers were able to accumulate enough money to have a savings account and to buy a home. Thernstrom attributed the paradoxical combination of relatively impressive property mobility and relatively modest occupational mobility to, first, the fact that the workers' children left school early to increase the family earning power, thereby sacrificing their own career opportunities; and second, to the likelihood that the peasant hunger for property reduced the possibility of investment in business.[3]

The unskilled laborers of Newburyport came from poor beginnings in Ireland or from New England subsistence farms, so they may have felt "a new sense of security and dignity" even though their occupational progress was "decidedly modest." In light of their limited aspirations, the workers "could view America as a land of opportunity despite the fact that the class realities which governed their life chances confined most of them to the working class." Though the workers experienced "a good deal of occupational mobility, only in rare cases was it mobility very far up the social ladder. The occupational structure was fluid to some degree, but the barriers against moving more than one notch upward were fairly high." His conclusion, suggesting that certain "class realities" were more powerful than the rags-to-riches mythology admitted, challenged the then popular notion of nineteenth-century America as a wide open, classless society.[4]

Thernstrom's rather bleak reassessment of the opportunities of those at the bottom reinforced the findings of some other scholars, such as William Miller, who had examined the social origins of those at the top and concluded that mobility was, for the most part, a myth "more conspicuous in American history books than in American history." Miller's study of the progressive era business elite, for instance, found that rich native-born Protestants controlled the top corporate positions and were likely to be succeeded by others like themselves; no more than 3 percent of the business elite came from immigrant or poor rural backgrounds.[5]

However, during the past decade, a number of historians have challenged both Thernstrom's view from the bottom and Miller's view from the top, and Thernstrom himself has revised his earlier views. In 1969, Herbert G. Gutman criticized the new conventional wisdom that the rags-to-riches theme was only myth. Gutman examined the social origins of the locomotive, iron, and machinery manufacturers in Paterson, New Jersey, and discovered that most of them had begun as skilled workers or apprentices. He pointed out that Miller's study relied on the very narrow national elite that gets listed in the Dictionary of American Biography or the National Cyclopedia of American Biography. He contended that there were thousands of successful businessmen who did not appear in these highly selective works but were nonetheless successful in their own communities. Gutman held that

What matters for purposes of this study is the fact that the rags-to-riches promise was not a mere myth in Paterson, New Jersey, between 1830 and 1880. So many successful manufacturers who had begun as workers walked the streets of that city then that it is not hard to believe that others less successful or just starting out on the lower rungs of the occupational mobility ladder could be convinced by personal knowledge that "hard work" resulted in spectacular material and social improvement.[6]

Other studies, using Thernstrom's Newburyport book as a reference point, found greater upward mobility among workers than Thernstrom had and suggested by contrast that Newburyport had an unusually sluggish economy. Clyde Griffen in 1969 examined Poughkeepsie records from 1850 to 1880 and unearthed impressive evidence of property accumulation by Irish laborers. But unlike Thernstrom's laborers, the Irish workers of Poughkeepsie did not increase their property holdings by taking their children out of school and putting them to work. Indeed, there was no significant difference between the major nationality groups in the percentage of children attending school or in the number of years that children stayed in school. Griffen concluded that "for the many small cities in America with comparably diversified economies and populations, local experience confirmed the national faith that merit sooner or later was rewarded by success."[7]

Paul B. Worthman in 1971 found striking upward mobility for white workers in Birmingham, Alabama, from 1880 to 1914:

Among unskilled white workers, movement from the bottom of the industrial pyramid occurred rapidly for those remaining in Birmingham. More than one-half of all three groups of unskilled white workingmen sampled who remained in the city for ten years climbed up the occupational ladder. For other white occupational categories, upward mobility was not so dramatic, although still substantial. Over a five or ten year period, one-quarter to one-third of the workers in most of the groups sampled who continued to work in Birmingham improved in their occupational status. After twenty years, almost one-half of the white skilled and semi-skilled workmen had experienced upward mobility.

Furthermore, movement from blue-collar to white-collar positions was extensive. In one sample, one-quarter of the workers who remained in the city a decade rose out of the working class; after twenty years, more than half had climbed to nonmanual jobs. A group sampled in 1899 experienced even more dramatic upward mobility, with one-third of them moving into nonmanual jobs within a decade. Nonmanual employment "generally consisted of employment as clerks, salesmen, policemen, or insurance agents." Some became building contractors, grocers, barbers, tailors, shoemakers, and mechanics, who, after accumulating a small amount of capital, went into business for themselves. Not surprisingly, given racially discriminatory laws and customs in Birmingham, blacks had much less upward mobility than whites. Worthman reported that "while 31 to 40% of Birmingham's white workingmen who remained in the city a decade were upwardly mobile, only 8 to 17% of persisting black workmen were this successful." After twenty years, one-third to one-half of white workers had moved up, but only one in six black workers. Still, there was some progress. Black barbers and shoemakers were able to open their own shops, and Worthman found "surprising" mobility among unskilled black workers: "Almost 20% of black unskilled sampled who remained in Birmingham a decade rose out of this category, and after 20 years almost 33% of them had succeeded in escaping this category. Between 1890 and 1909, moreover, 38% of the black unskilled workers still in Birmingham in the latter year had even risen to nonmanual employment." However, few blacks managed to obtain much property, and black workers experienced higher rates of downward mobility than whites; since black workers were "constantly pushed out of various occupations toward the bottom of the occupational hierarchy," whatever gains they made were precarious.[8]

Like Worthman, Richard J. Hopkins documented strong racial differentials in Atlanta, Georgia, from 1870 to 1910. He noted that "color was more important than ethnic background in determining who could improve his occupational status and who could not." But among white workers, regardless of nativity, upward mobility was striking, inasmuch as one of every five white manual workers, both native and immigrant, moved up into white-collar jobs. Hopkins observed that "the achievement of some degree of success or improvement in occupational status was fairly common [for both native and immigrant] white Atlantans in the later nineteenth century."[9]

Michael P. Weber specifically compared the workers of

Newburyport to those of Warren, Pennsylvania, and held that Warren's workers enjoyed much greater occupational success: "Warren's unskilled workers became skilled craftsmen and nonmanual workers with marked regularity. Between one-third and one-half of all unskilled laborers of the 1880 census group managed to achieve white-collar status." Weber concluded that

a fluid occupational structure and considerable economic opportunity accompanied the industrialization and urbanization of Warren. Large numbers of workers migrated in and out of the community each decade, but those who remained often advanced into higher level occupations. Clearly, few workers experienced the spectacular mobility enjoyed by the heroes in the novels of Horatio Alger, but middle-class occupations became a distinct possibility. For the workers of Warren, the promise of mobility was a reality enjoyed by many.[10]

In *The Golden Door: Italian and Jewish Immigrant Mobility in New York City, 1880–1915*, Thomas Kessner held that there was greater upward mobility in New York City than in any other American city that had been analyzed thus far. He established mobility rates for Jews and Italians and maintained that "social mobility was both rapid and widespread even for immigrants who came from the peasant towns of southern Italy and the Russian pale." In the decade from 1880 to 1890, the rate of movement from blue- to white-collar occupations was 22 percent in Atlanta, 21 percent in Omaha, and 12 percent in Boston, averages that included both natives and immigrants. According to Kessner, the Jews and Italians in New York City "who began the decade at the bottom of the Promised City's social order, rose out of the manual class at a rate of 37% in the same decade." While Kessner does not specifically examine the connection between occupational mobility and schooling (nor do any of the other studies), he notes that "Jewish offspring born in America and open to its training and schools did better than their European-born brethren and subsequently moved up the ladder more quickly."[11]

Of more significance than any of the studies that have appeared since Thernstrom's *Poverty and Progress*, which is better known than they are, are the revisions that Thernstrom himself has made. In an essay published in 1972, he acknowledged that his "early work—on the laborers in Newburyport—was misleading in its emphasis on the barriers to working class occupational achievement. . . . In other communities . . . the occupational horizon was notably more open."[12]

In 1973, Thernstrom published *The Other Bostonians: Poverty and Progress in the American Metropolis, 1880–1970*, a landmark study of patterns of migration and social mobility which is unusual for its comprehensiveness and its breadth. Never before have these issues been tested in so large a metropolis over so long a period of time. His choice of a major city and his decision to cover nearly a century and to include the entire occupational structure, rather than just the lowest strata of the working class, represented recognition of the limitations of the New-buryport study. In Newburyport, Thernstrom had focused on unskilled laborers, most of whom were newly arrived Irish Catholic immigrants, over a thirty-year period. He could not be sure that what was true for those at the bottom of the ladder was representative of workers in general, whether the stagnant Newburyport economy was typical of growing urban centers, and whether the brevity of the period he studied made it impossible to discern long-term trends or cyclical fluctuations in mobility rates. The Boston study was designed to avoid these uncertainties.[13]

Thernstrom's Boston conclusions are indeed a sharp correction of the pessimistic Newburyport findings. Both as a revision of earlier work and as the most extensive mobility research yet assembled, *The Other Bostonians* is of special significance.

Thernstrom's central finding is that, throughout the period from 1880 to 1970, there was "a great deal of upward career mobility for men situated on the lower rungs of the class ladder," and considerably less downward mobility for those in white-collar occupations. Blue-collar workers were not trapped at the bottom of the occupational structure, as radical historians allege. Indeed, Thernstrom found that "lower levels of the community occupational structure were strikingly fluid." Within even a single decade, more than a third of blue-collar workers improved their occupational position. Forty percent or more of semiskilled workers and one-third of the entirely unskilled eventually became either skilled craftsmen or white-collar workers. Further, about one of every four blue-collar workers moved up into white-collar jobs during their careers. Much to his surprise, Thernstrom observed that "mobility into non-manual jobs was no more difficult for semiskilled than for skilled workers, and only a little more difficult for un-skilled laborers."[14]

Prior social advantage or disadvantage proved to be important, though not to the extent that the radical historians suggest. Those who reached the high white-collar stratum tended to stay there, to be followed by 90 percent of their sons. This is not remarkable, since someone who becomes a professional or a substantial businessman is unlikely to slip into blue-collar work and is likely to guide his children into similar professional pursuits. While the haves were protected from much downward mobility, the have-nots did not simply inherit their fathers' status: four out of ten blue-collar sons ended up in white-collar jobs, and six out of ten children of unskilled or semiskilled workers rose to become either skilled craftsmen or white-collar workers. Interestingly, the competition for occupational gains was not a "zero-sum game, in which one party's gains are necessarily matched by another party's losses." The movement up of a blue-collar worker did not mean the movement down of a white-collar worker; there was evidently more room at the top as the economy became more industrialized. With respect to mobility, Thernstrom notes, "the community seems to have had the best of all possible worlds, with lots of the desirable kind (upward) and a much lower volume of the undesirable kind (downward)."[15]

Social origins counted heavily in times of economic catastrophe. In especially serious economic depressions, the access of unskilled and semiskilled workers to better jobs was sharply reduced, and these setbacks sometimes meant a permanent handicap of career opportunities. The effect of economic depression on the upward movement of skilled workers and white-collar workers was, by contrast, minimal and temporary.

Despite the differential impact of social origins, wrote Thernstrom,

children born into the working class were very far from being doomed to die in the working class. The odds of climbing into a white-collar job were only a shade less than even. And the chance that a youth whose father stood at the very bottom of the occupational ladder, in a menial unskilled or semiskilled job, would rise to a higher occupation himself—either skilled or white collar—was actually better than even. The background advantages of men from middle-class families were substantial; opportunities to rise in the world for men from working-class homes were also substantial.[16]

From the mass of data assembled for this study, Thernstrom was able to discount the popular notion that the poor are locked into a vicious, inevitable cycle of poverty that is transmitted across generations. A clear majority of poor youths climbed to a higher occupational level than their fathers: "That upward mobility was more common than the transmission of low-skilled status from one generation to the next was a fact of profound significance. Doubtless poverty did breed poverty in some instances, but over the span of nearly a century the Boston social order has been sufficiently fluid to make that more the exception than the rule."[17]

Nor was the ghetto a rigidly segregated community for the foreign-born. While there were distinct ethnic neighborhoods, the individuals in them were constantly changing, moving in and out again. Thomas Kessner, in his study of New York City's Italians and Jews, argued that the ethnic ghetto was not a barrier to mobility at all, but rather that it was a "mobility launcher," a community where the immigrant could find friends and countrymen, a familiar place of worship, special foods, and a grapevine of information about where to find a job or a place to live.[18]

In *Poverty and Progress*, Thernstrom had pointed to the handicapping effect of discrimination against foreign-born laborers, since their occupational progress was substantially less than that of native-born laborers. But the findings of his 90-year study proved more complicated than the message that emerged from the 30-year study, and in *The Other Bostonians* Thernstrom qualified his earlier view:

It is true that the climb up the class ladder was harder for men of foreign stock than for Yankees, and harder for some immigrant groups than for others. But part of the explanation, at least, was not simple prejudice or even passive structural discrimination but objective differences in qualifications to perform demanding occupational tasks. And all of the major immigrant groups, however dismal their plight when they first arrived, experienced substantial upward mobility in subsequent years.[19]

Thernstrom concluded that "the American class system . . . allowed substantial privilege for the privileged and extensive opportunity for the underprivileged. . . ." The social structure was not perfectly open; initial advantages and disadvantages did influence people's occupational chances. But "neither those who boasted that America was a land of endless opportunity nor their critics who insisted that the deck was stacked against the poor were entirely correct." He suspects that future research will show that the American social order was "distinctly more fluid than that of most European countries," and that the broad availability of opportunity inhibited the formation of class consciousness or class-based protest movements.[20]

It is only during the past dozen or so years that historians' use of computers has made it possible to work with large-scale survey data and to investigate social mobility patterns in the distant past. As the technology becomes more sophisticated and as urban historians become more inventive in their application of the technology, the present state of knowledge may be qualified, verified, or reversed altogether. But, pending further research, it does appear that upward social mobility trends have been established in certain American cities during the nineteenth and early twentieth centuries.

No such conclusion, however, can be drawn about the role of the school in promoting or hindering upward mobility during the same period. The radical historians have little specific evidence to substantiate their claims about the school's impotence. Katz describes industrial education, the kindergarten, and vocational guidance as innovations that inhibited social mobility by acting as social sorting devices. Industrial education, he writes, instilled "the attitudes and skills appropriate to manual working-class status. Regardless of the rhetoric of its sponsors, industrial education has proved to be an ingenious way of providing universal secondary schooling without disturbing the shape of the social structure and without permitting excessive amounts of social mobility." But he offers no empirical data as to how many children were in an industrial education curriculum, what happened to them subsequently, or whether, in its absence, the same children would have been working in sweatshops.[21]

Colin Greer titles one of his chapters "The Assimilation of the Immigrants: The School Didn't Do It." But he doesn't know that the school "didn't do it," because he offers no evidence to disentangle the influence of the school from other social and economic factors. What he actually seems to be saying is that neither the school nor anything else in American life helped the immigrants succeed because he believes that "the story of immigrant success is a legend too." If the immigrants didn't succeed, then the schools can't have been responsible for their success. Those few groups that did break into the middle class, he insists, did not make it because of their high academic achievement. But it is never clear why he is so certain about the irrelevance of their schooling. All that he proves is what was already well known to historians and social scientists: "Some groups did better than others, and some parts of some groups did best of all . . . [and] some groups did less well than others, and some parts of some groups did worst of all." David Tyack reviewed Greer's assertions about the impotence of the school and wrote, "It appears that only those who make claims about the *positive* influences of the public schools have to meet precise scholarly standards of proof."[22]

Thus, the assertions by Katz, Greer, Spring, Karier, and the others about the relationship between education and social mobility in the nineteenth and early twentieth centuries are so far no more than assertions, and, what is more, they are assertions grounded on the incorrect belief that there was very little or no upward mobility in the past. They freely charge that the schools inhibited mobility but the evidence—negative or positive—to prove the effect of education on social mobility in the past just is not available. Historians are presently trying to establish the nature of the relationship, but the data are fragmentary in some ways, voluminous in others, and generally difficult to assemble. Even when school records for individuals are located and compared to census data, tax rolls, and other information, factoring out the precise influence of the schools, as against a host of other unidentified elements, is extremely problematic.

It appears, then, that the present state of historical knowledge points to two conclusions about the past: first, that there has been significant upward mobility in American society; and second, that the relative importance of schooling in this process is thus far uncertain. Popular notions are not very different from these findings. Perhaps the persistence of the American belief in the possibility of upward mobility, of "making it," is due to the remembered family history of middle-class Americans whose own parents or grandparents were poor. The transition from rags-to-shirtsleeves in one, two, or three generations was not uncommon. It is also commonplace to hear this rise in status attributed not just to schooling but to such unmeasurable factors as hard work, determination, and good luck. Further research is needed to clarify the relative influence of schooling, as well as the reciprocal relationship between schooling and social structure.

But whatever conclusions are reached about the past, the objection might reasonably be raised that American society has become less open in the modern period, that the growth of large corporations and the decline of small businesses imply an increasingly rigid class structure whose lines are less easily crossed now than 50 or 100 years ago. Or, as several of the revisionists maintain (agreeing by default with Richard Herrnstein), the signal importance of the school as a stratifying device might actually decrease upward mobility by establishing a meritocracy, a caste system based on intelligence and credentials. And if, as Bowles and Gintis hold, the reason that "higher levels of schooling and economic success tend to go together" is that those who are already economically advantaged get more years of schooling, then schooling is a means of preventing upward mobility. And if, as they assert, the schools merely reproduce the class structure by conferring educational rewards on those who already have high economic position, then one would expect to find very little upward mobility at all. What their argument amounts to is that the rich get rich and the poor get poorer, and the educational system makes it all appear just.[23]

However, the weight of available evidence runs counter to the radicals' beliefs that American society has become more rigid and class-bound in the modern period and that schooling deters upward mobility. Stephan Thernstrom's previously described long-term study of the occupational structure in Boston found that the opportunities for upward advancement remained "excellent" and surprisingly stable from 1880 until the present, and that, "despite automation, rising educational requirements for many jobs, the emergence of giant corporate bureaucracies, and other massive changes in American society . . . no clear trend toward a more rigid and constricted social structure was visible." Thernstrom's rebuttal of the radical hypothesis is especially significant because many of them rely on his earlier work, and because Thernstrom was sufficiently sympathetic to their views to have written the introduction to one of the radical histories.[24]

Unlike historians, who thus far lack sufficient data to state conclusively how education affected the social structure in the past, contemporary sociologists do claim to have established that formal schooling contributes directly to upward mobility and that American society continues to have a high rate of upward mobility in its occupational structure.

The most comprehensive study of these issues is Peter

Blau and Otis Dudley Duncan's *The American Occupational Structure,* which reported the results of an intergenerational survey based on a national sample of 20,000 men in 1962. Blau and Duncan found that "there is a large amount of upward mobility in the American occupational structure. Upward movements far exceed downward movements, whether raw numbers, percentages or departures from standardized expectations are considered. . . . Sons from all occupational origins participate in this predominant upward movement."[25]

Education is not irrelevant to mobility, according to Blau and Duncan:

The chances of upward mobility are directly related to education. . . . The proportion of men who experience some upward mobility increases steadily with education from a low of 12 per cent for those reporting no schooling to a high of 76 per cent for those who have gone beyond college. The proportion who have moved up a long distance from their social origins increases in the same regular fashion from under 8 per cent for those with less than five years of schooling to 53 per cent for those with some postgraduate work.[26]

Their evidence refutes those who contend that education simply reproduces the existing social order by rewarding those with high family status. They demonstrate statistically that, while family position is associated with education,

of the total or gross effect of education on occupational status in 1962, only a minor part of it consists in a transmission of the prior influence of "family position". . . . Far from serving in the main as a factor perpetuating initial status, education operates *primarily* to induce variation in occupational status that is independent of initial status.[27]

In other words, education has a substantial effect on occupational achievement that is independent of one's social origins.

Comparing social mobility rates of the United States and other industrialized countries, Blau and Duncan found that, in most categories, the United States offered the greatest upward social mobility. Upward movement from the working class into the elite stratum, for instance, was highest in the United States; nearly 10 percent of sons whose fathers were manual workers moved into the most elite occupations, a higher proportion than in any other industrialized country.[28]

Other studies reinforce Blau and Duncan's conclusion that there is "no evidence of 'rigidification' " in terms of social and economic opportunities. A 1964 survey of the social origins of big-business executives showed that entry to the top echelons of American business was more open than at any time in the past. Updating Mabel Newcomer's 1950 analysis of the big-business executive, the 1964 study reported that "only 10.5 percent of the current generation of big-business executives . . . are sons of wealthy families; as recently as 1950 the corresponding figure was 36.1 percent, and at the turn of the century, 45.6 percent."[29]

Similar conclusions are reached in Christopher Jencks' *Inequality.* He finds that

there is still an enormous amount of economic mobility from one generation to the next. Indeed, there is nearly as much economic inequality among brothers raised in the same homes as in the general population. This means that inequality is recreated anew in each generation, even among people who start life in essentially identical circumstances.

He notes that "men who get a lot of education are likely to end up in high-status occupations, even if their fathers worked in low-status occupations." Family background is not "the primary determinant of status," since brothers differ in status almost as much as random individuals. On the contrary, he reports that "men with the same amount of education have occupations that are even more alike than men who have the same parents." He holds that "educational attainment is one of the prime determinants of occupational status," though "there are still enormous status differences among people with the same amount of education." One of his findings is that

schooling seems to be important in and of itself, not as a proxy for cognitive skills or family background. Both family background and cognitive skills help a man get through school, but beyond that they have very little direct influence on status. Years of schooling, in contrast, have a substantial influence, even when we compare individuals from identical backgrounds and with identical cognitive skills.[30]

The importance of educational attainment, he suspects, is due to employers' use of educational credentials as rationing devices for good jobs. His own preference, however, is not for a society with maximum social mobility (or equality of opportunity), but for one where rewards are equal (or equality of results). Schools help people get an equal chance to win unequal rewards.

But Jencks wants to reduce inequality, not just to randomize it; his concern is that even when there is complete equality of opportunity, gross discrepancies of wealth and income remain. He believes that the United States should shift from an ideology of equal opportunity to one of equal results. To achieve this would require an extensive program of governmental regimentation and control of the population. Aside from massive income redistribution, Jencks proposes governmental regulation of wages and working conditions, and some sort of national or international machinery to prevent unusually valuable workers from finding a way to gain special privileges.

To insure job equality within each organization, the government might require rotation of management jobs between the competent and the less competent. Those who got more than their "share" of higher education might get an income-tax surcharge, while those who got less than their "share" might get a subsidy or lower taxes. What appears to some people as the pursuit of excellence in academic life or the pursuit of efficiency and productivity in the work-place strikes him as the perpetuation of inequality. His line of reasoning is predicated on the proposition that equality of opportunity should be repudiated because it presumes the continuation of inequality among individuals.

The fundamental question underlying the discussion of social mobility is the definition of equality, and during the past decade a vigorous debate has ensued about the contrasting goals of equal opportunity and equal results. The basic question is this: Should the United States be a society in which everyone has an equal chance to succeed or a society in which everyone has an equal share of income, status, and power? The idea of social mobility, like that of equal opportunity, suggests that individuals succeed according to their individual merits and that others do not succeed for lack of those same qualities. Those who argue on behalf of equal results find the very idea of social competition objectionable and prefer a society in which there is no social ladder, no social class distinction, no striving for unequal shares of status and income.[31]

The concept of equal opportunity is a fundamental tenet of classical liberalism; it presumes that the individual is the basic unit of society, not the group. Thus, each individual has equal rights before the law, is entitled to equal treatment by government, and is to be neither favored nor handicapped by group affiliation (such as race, religion, sex, family background, etc.). The society that values equal opportunity puts a premium on talent, energy, and excellence by rewarding individual attainment. And the encouragement of initiative and innovation has in no small measure contributed to the extraordinary productivity of the American economic system, which has achieved the highest standard of living ever known in the world.

But the critics of equal opportunity have multiplied during the past decade, and they include (among others) Christopher Jencks and John Rawls (who wrote a lengthy philosophical treatise arguing that justice should be defined as equality in its strictest sense). The problem with equality of opportunity, in the eyes of the critics, is that it can be construed as social Darwinism, a political justification for the survival of the fittest and callous disregard of the unfittest. Thus, Jencks holds that equal opportunity allows, indeed encourages, an unequal distribution of income; he advocates income redistribution to equalize the rewards available to the smart and the dumb, the lazy and the ambitious, the lucky and the unlucky. Thus, the Coleman Report (the Equal Educational Opportunity Survey of 1966) showed that mostly white and mostly black schools were nearly equal in resources but grossly unequal in results (academic achievement) and diverted the discussion of educational policy away from how to achieve equal opportunity to how to achieve equal results. Thus, civil rights groups have shifted their strategy from one of equal opportunity to one of equal results: instead of demanding that universities and employers eliminate race as a factor in admission or employment, they now insist that race be specifically considered in deciding whom to employ or admit.

Actually, the terms of the discussion are distorted by setting up a simple contradiction between equal opportunity and equal results, because in doing so, equal opportunity is cast as a laissez faire, brutal competition and equal results are portrayed as the goal of humanistic, unselfish people. What is lost when this false dichotomy is posed is, first, the extent to which both concepts are merged in American social policy, and second, the social cost of adopting equal-results policies at the expense of equal opportunity policies.

Christopher Jencks notes with some dismay that most Americans are committed to the principle of equal opportunity, and not to the sort of egalitarian socialism that he favors. Opinion polls have shown that Americans don't really mind differences in income, that they like to think that there is a possibility of their striking it rich someday, that they admire risk-taking, that they want to be able to pass along some of what they have earned to their children. By their market behavior, Americans show that they prefer to spend their excess earnings on status symbols like cars, boats, and eight-track stereos—on their avocations and vacations. Election results have shown that Americans generally find confiscatory taxes unacceptable, and that they prefer to spend their excess income on their own wants rather than on other people's needs.

On the other hand, despite popular resistance to high taxes and egalitarianism, governmental policies do include an extensive combination of both equal opportunity and equal results. Every governmental social program is a form of intervention that runs counter to laissez faire principles, and every transfer program is an effort to redress inequalities. The money spent for food stamps, welfare, medical assistance, public housing, aid to education, community development, and so on, is intended to improve the condition of those who have not succeeded in the competition of equal opportunity. Public universities have been vastly enlarged so that a college education would be available to all who want it, not just to those who win the competition for admission. The income tax, insofar as it is progressive, is a redistributive mechanism.

Those who propose radical egalitarian measures do so because they value equality more than they value either liberty or efficiency. Full egalitarianism could be achieved only by establishing a powerful state bureaucracy capable of constantly monitoring the redistribution of money, jobs, and other rewards. One consequence of such policies is the creation of a new class of bureaucrats in the theoretically classless society; this enlargement of the state bureaucracy and its necessary absorption of the private sector are threatening possibilities in light of the history of totalitarianism in the twentieth century. Political rights and freedoms have not fared well in nations where the power of the state is not checked by a healthy, pluralistic private sector.

Additionally, an egalitarian distribution of incomes would have a depressing effect on productivity, since economic incentives would have to be abandoned. By cutting the pie into equal slices, the total size of the pie would shrink; more equality means more inefficiency, because there would be no incentive to work harder or to be more efficient or to achieve excellence, since good work and bad work would get equal rewards. In the American economic system, there are built-in incentives for the producer to be more efficient, more innovative, less costly, and more pleasing to consumers than the competition. In a planned society, the planners decide what the consumer should have, where people should work, and how their jobs should be performed.

But the American system is not an example of free market capitalism where respect for liberty and efficiency overwhelms any concern for equality. Liberal democracy in the modern era has been posited on the belief that equality must be balanced with liberty and efficiency, and that none of these values should be jeopardized by the others. There are and will continue to be elements of both equality of opportunity and egalitarianism in American social policy, and the question for the future is how these concepts will be adjusted to each other. Just as equal opportunity in its most extreme form would be anathema because of the suffering that would result, so too would pure egalitarianism be a horror because of the destruction of privacy, liberty, and individualism that would be necessary.

CHAPTER SIX

Education Still Matters

Until very recently, equality of opportunity was no more than a distant, visionary goal. For some Americans, it has still not been attained. This is a point that radical critics stress, and it is the basis for their charge that the exclusion of certain groups is a systematic, structural defect in American society, which the schools are either partially responsible for or are powerless to change.

No reasonable person can fail to acknowledge the inequities of the past and present and the human devastation caused by prejudice and discrimination. But it is also reasonable to seek to ascertain whether there is a trend toward correction of the injustices of the past. The important question is not whether there was racism and exploitation in the past, for clearly there was; the question, rather, is whether American society is getting better or worse or remaining the same for those who have been victimized in the past.

Are white ethnic minorities systematically disadvantaged, for example? Blau and Duncan found that "the occupational opportunities of white ethnic minorities on the whole differ little from those of whites of native parentage." And, they added parenthetically, "indeed, they are considerably superior to those of southern whites." The difference between these two groups, interestingly, was attributed to the lesser educational attainment of southern whites, which reconfirms the importance of education in occupational achievement. What is more, according to Blau and Duncan, "sons of immigrants who live in the region of their birth tend to achieve an occupational status that is superior to that of comparable natives, not only if they descend from more prestigeful, but also if they descend from less prestigeful nationalities."[1]

It is important to document the fact that discrimination against religious and ethnic minorities existed in the past, but it is no less important to determine whether the handicaps of the past are being overcome. Andrew Greeley reported recently that the descendants of what formerly were the most disadvantaged white minorities have surpassed the white Anglo-Saxon Protestant groups in terms of income. The highest average incomes were those of Jews, Irish Catholics, Italian Catholics, German Catholics, and Polish Catholics, in that order. Episcopalians and Presbyterians followed the "new immigrant" groups on the national income ladder.[2]

While white minorities may have largely overcome the discrimination of the past, the picture is sharply different for blacks. Blau and Duncan reported that blacks were handicapped "by having poorer parents, less education and inferior early career experiences than whites." And even when these handicaps were statistically controlled, the black man's occupational chances were still consistently inferior to those of whites. Because of racism, blacks suffered "profound inequalities of occupational opportunities." Furthermore, blacks with the same education as whites did not achieve as much occupationally, nor were they likely to be paid the same in equivalent occupations.[3]

Educational investment did not have the same economic return for blacks in 1962 as for whites, except at the highest levels of educational attainment. The difference between white and black income grew with increasing levels of education, except for the most highly educated; the largest income differential was between white and black men who had some college; and the smallest differential was between those whites and blacks with the least education, as well as those whites and blacks with the most education. Blau and Duncan concluded that "the fact that Negroes obtain fewer rewards than the majority group for their educational investments, robbing them of important incentives to incur these costs, may help explain why many Negroes exhibit little interest or motivation in pursuing their education." In this context, dropping out of school was economically rational behavior for blacks.[4]

These findings were based on data gathered in 1962, before the passage of major civil rights legislation and before the launching of the "Great Society" social programs in 1964–1965. Whether or not these initiatives improved the status of black Americans has an important bearing on the validity or invalidity of the radical case against liberal meliorism. Bowles and Gintis state that liberal social policy was "decisively discredited" by its ineffectiveness in the late 1960s. Clarence Karier, finding no diminution in white racism, paints a bleak picture of the prospects for blacks:

With the collapse of desegregation efforts as well as compulsory [sic] education programs, the dangers, for white racists, of an integrated American society passed as blacks were increasingly confined below the poverty level in economically segregated, decaying urban ghettos. Further, with the withdrawal of federal support for urban schools and the consequent deterioration of these schools as educational institutions, the future for black youth was sealed.[5]

While Karier maintains that "all history is written from a perspective that is invariably shaped out of one's existential present," and that "each researcher's ideology determines his approach to the data," still there are some factual questions that can be resolved regardless of the researcher's ideology. How one appraises John Dewey's philosophy is a matter of opinion, but whether or not compensatory programs were "drastically reduced," as Karier elsewhere claims, is a matter of fact. The major federal compensatory program, Title I of the Elementary and Secondary Education Act, received approximately $1.05 billion in 1967; the same program was funded at $1.5 billion in 1973 and 1974, and at $1.9 billion in 1975. Whether or not these funds were apportioned well or spent well are separate issues; the point is that the amount appropriated by the federal government was not "drastically reduced."[6]

Are blacks "increasingly confined below the poverty level in economically segregated, decaying urban ghettos"? According to the Census Bureau, 58.3 percent of American blacks were living in central cities in 1974. This represented a significant increase over 1960, when about 52 percent of blacks lived in central cities. Some of this growth reflects natural increase, and some is due to an inflow of population from rural areas to cities during the 1960s. The implications of this concentration are mixed, and not altogether negative. It suggests, for instance, that blacks will be able to forge a base of political power in the cities. Clusters of black voters elect black mayors, congressmen, and state legislators. From 1971 to 1975, the total number of black elected officials in the nation nearly doubled, from 1,860 to 3,503; of 135 black mayors, 11 were elected in large metropolitan cities. Political power means control over jobs, contracts, and policies, as well as better articulation of black interests.[7]

During the period from 1970 to 1974, black population growth in the central cities slowed to the level of natural increase; additionally, there was both a black immigration to the South and an increase by nearly 20 percent of the black suburban population. While blacks are now only 5 percent of the suburban population, the likeliest way to enlarge this proportion is through such liberal social policies as fair housing legislation, court action against restrictive zoning codes, and housing subsidies. Governmental policies can be shaped to encourage and preserve integrated neighborhoods, just as they have been used in the past for the opposite purpose. But building political consensus for liberal social policy among the electorate requires both a belief in the efficacy of such policies and a commitment to the democratic political process.[8]

Recent national census studies indicate that the liberal social policies of the Johnson Administration had a significant positive effect. In 1964, approximately half of all American blacks were below the poverty line; by 1974, the proportion had dropped to 31.4 percent. The most rapid decline in the number of poor blacks occurred during the late 1960s, a time when liberal social policies were implemented. During the period from 1964 to 1974, the proportion of black families earning over $15,000 annually grew from 9 percent to 19 percent; the period of fastest gain was from 1965 to 1970.[9]

The overall income gap between blacks and whites remains large, though it has narrowed. Black family income in 1974 was only 58 percent of white family income, compared to 54 percent in 1964. But poverty was not randomly spread among blacks. Young black families in the North and West, those in which both spouses were employed, had incomes that were 99 percent of the income of equivalent white families; even in the South, where black earnings were lowest, these families earned 87 percent of the income of corresponding white families. Black poverty was increasingly concentrated among female-headed families, which were two-thirds of all poor black families by 1974.[10]

The composite picture of social and economic trends for the past fifteen years does not support the radical claim that liberal social policy has been discredited. On the contrary, it appears to validate the effectiveness of a many-pronged attack on poverty and inequality, beginning with stringent civil rights laws and including governmental action on jobs, education, housing, and economic development. Similarly, certain Title I compensatory education programs produced measurable gains for disadvantaged children. As Ralph Tyler has noted, the widespread contrary impression—that better schooling can't make a difference—was based on the Coleman report and Christopher Jencks's *Inequality*, but in fact, neither study measured educational progress after the federal legislation of 1965 became operative. Indeed, the proposition that schools "don't make a difference" in terms of educational achievement has been widely challenged, particularly as a result of the decade-long investigations of the International Evaluation of Educational Achievement, which compared the results of schooling in nineteen countries. Alex Inkeles of Stanford University, reviewing the implications of these studies, wrote that

In the light of these findings we can see clearly how profoundly misled both educators and the public have become about a basic issue having major policy implications. Differentiation of family conditions clearly does not, in itself, decisively determine the academic performance of the child. The Coleman report, which has been the chief cause of a great deal of this confusion, states that once "the socioeconomic background of the students is taken into account" then "schools are remarkably similar in the way they relate to the achievement of their pupils" (Coleman, 1966, p. 21). The IEA data permit us drastically to revise this statement as follows: *After the socioeconomic background of the students has been taken into account, students are still remarkably different in their academic performance, with about 90% of the variance in their test scores still remaining to be explained by other factors.* (Italics in the original.)

These "other factors," Inkeles notes, may turn out to be "more sensitive measures of socioeconomic status," but even if the variance rose to as much as 20 percent, it would still leave 80 percent of student academic achievement unexplained by home background. In the IEA studies, school quality variables turned out to have "substantial" influence on achievement, and some analyses produced the finding that school quality was "of equal or of even greater importance than the home background of the child."[11]

Despite a spate of articles and books about the irrelevance of schooling, young blacks are staying in school longer than at any time in the past; their decision to seek more education is a rational response to the new political and social climate generated by effective liberal social policies which have opened up new opportunities for college-educated blacks. The rapid increase in black college enrollment during the past decade has been nothing less than phenomenal. From 1965 until 1976, black college enrollment grew by a remarkable 388 percent, from 274,000 to 1,062,000 (during the same period, white college enrollment was up by 61.5 percent). Blacks, who were 4.8 percent of all college students in 1965, were 10.7 percent of all college students by 1976 (in the latter year, blacks were 12.3 percent of the 18-24 year-old cohort). As the following figures show, the mid-1970s was a period in which the gap between the races in college enrollment was steadily reduced over a brief period:

College Enrollment for 18–21 Year-Olds, by Race

		TOTAL POPULATION	IN COLLEGE	PERCENT IN COLLEGE	GAP BETWEEN RACES
1973	White	12,702,000	4,146,000	32.6	13.3
	Black	1,852,000	358,000	19.3	
1974	White	13,157,000	4,248,000	32.3	10.5
	Black	1,896,000	413,000	21.8	
1975	White	13,448,000	4,655,000	34.6	9.7
	Black	1,997,000	497,000	24.9	
1976	White	13,642,000	4,685,000	34.3	7.5
	Black	2,067,000	554,000	26.8	

A narrowing of racial differentials may also be seen in the rate of college enrollment among the total population under the age of 35. Among whites, 7.7 percent of that age group was enrolled in college in 1973, compared to 4.9 percent of blacks; by 1976, white enrollment had risen to 8.9 percent, while black enrollment had increased to 7.2 percent. It is interesting to note, too, that an identical 17 percent of both white and black families below the poverty line reported at least one family member in college.[12]

This massive movement of blacks into college is of great importance in the effort to achieve racial equality, since a college education is essential as preparation for professional, technical, and scientific occupations. The educational and occupational gains of blacks since the passage of the 1964 Civil Rights Act have been fully documented by Richard B. Freeman in a report for the Carnegie Commission on Higher Education titled *Black Elite: The New Market for Highly Educated Black Americans*. The Freeman report is a comprehensive summary of how blacks have been affected by the legal, political, economic, and social transformation of American society since 1964. Its central finding is that blacks have made remarkable progress in income, occupation, and education. The most dramatic gains were made by young college graduates, who have achieved full economic equality with their white peers.[13]

Freeman has found that the occupational profile of black workers has begun to converge with that of whites, as black women move out of domestic jobs and into factory and clerical work, and as black men move increasingly into professional, craft, and managerial jobs. Among college graduates, this convergence was even more pronounced, as young blacks moved into fields that had been traditionally closed to blacks, like law, management, engineering, accounting, and medicine. And for the first time in history, young black professionals began their careers on an equal footing with nonblacks; according to Freeman,

Census statistics on income, special survey data from southern black colleges . . . and interviews with college placement directors at those institutions reveal a collapse in labor market discrimination against starting black male graduates in the late 1960s, which, if continued, marks the end of discrimination in high-level labor markets.[14]

Furthermore, Freeman canvassed twenty-two southern black colleges and learned that all had experienced an enormous increase in the recruitment activities of major corporations on their campuses. In 1960, the average number of business recruiters at each campus was 4; in fact, eleven of the colleges had no visits from corporate representatives that year. By 1970, the average black southern campus reported an average of 297 visits by corporate recruiters. North Carolina Agricultural and Technical State

University, which had been visited by only 6 recruiters in 1960, received 517 in 1970; Atlanta University's recruiters increased from none to 510. The placement directors of the black colleges also reported that their graduates, beginning in the late 1960s, were being offered the same starting salaries that were paid to others in the same field, a sharp contrast with earlier practices in the labor market.[15]

The new market for black college graduates was translated very quickly into substantial income gains. As recently as 1959, the typical young black male college graduate earned less than the typical white male *high school* graduate. By 1973, the young black college graduate (age twenty-five to twenty-nine) was earning *more* than the equivalent white college graduate. Black women had achieved income parity with whites much earlier; income for female college graduates, regardless of race, was roughly the same by 1959, as it was for all female high school graduates by 1969. By 1973, black female college graduates and black high school graduates were earning *more* than their white peers. Freeman notes that the major occupational disadvantages of black women "result from sexual rather than racial differences in market opportunities."[16]

Freeman's analyses reveal that blacks received a significantly higher return on their investment in higher education than whites did, and this held true both for college and graduate study. In 1973, young black college men earned nearly $3,500 more than blacks who had only graduated high school, while the differential for young white men between a college degree and a high school diploma was then only $540 in annual earnings. The income premium for blacks was six times that for whites, with the result that the economic incentive for black men to go to college was considerably higher than it was for whites.[17]

Similarly, blacks with graduate training obtained greater increases in income than did comparable whites and therefore had greater economic incentive for investment in graduate study. While the earnings of whites with graduate training exceeded that of blacks in almost every age category, the economic return on black investment was higher than it was for whites. Black men with five or more years of college earned $3,103 more per year than those with only four years (a 36 percent income advantage), while whites with graduate training earned $1,920 more than those with four years of college (a 13 percent gain).[18]

Among black and white women, the economic advantage of getting graduate training was nearly the same (and slightly in favor of black women), but black women in every age category under fifty-five earned more than white women, whether they had four years of college or graduate training. In response to these changes, Freeman notes, the number of black graduate students nearly doubled between 1967 and 1973.[19]

During this unusual period of black educational and occupational progress, certain traditional patterns were reversed:

- As late as 1964, most black students attended predominantly black colleges; by 1970, three-quarters of black college students were enrolled in predominantly white colleges.
- Blau and Duncan had reported a difference between white and black incomes that grew larger with increasing levels of education, so that the largest income differential was between whites and blacks with some college; Freeman concludes that this pattern was shattered during the late 1960s.

- Because of racial discrimination in the occupational structure, nearly half of all black professionals traditionally went into teaching. By 1975, according to Freeman, the career plans of black college students and graduates were very similar to those of whites; only about 10 percent intended to go into education, while 20 percent or more planned to go into business and others planned to be doctors (6.3 percent), lawyers (8.9 percent), engineers (8.3 percent), and scientists (2.2 percent).

- Sociologists had noted in the past that black families had been unable to pass along their socioeconomic gains to their children; this, however, changed in the 1960s as the children of better educated, more prosperous blacks went in growing numbers to college.[20]

As a result of the dramatic gains of the late 1960s and early 1970s, those blacks who are under thirty-five, well educated, and middle-class have achieved virtually full economic equality with their white peers. What this means is not simply economic benefit for this group alone; it means that, for the first time in American history, blacks can achieve equality through some of the same mechanisms that other groups have used and from which blacks have previously been excluded. Schooling is one of those mechanisms, and its importance has grown as the American economy has become more complex and technical. For the first time, black investment in education is worth making. Just as dropping out was once an economically rational decision, getting more education is now as rational for blacks as it has been for whites.

Further confirmation of the relationship between schooling and occupational achievement has come from Robert M. Hauser and David L. Featherman, sociologists at the University of Wisconsin who recently completed the first systematic replication of the Blau and Duncan study of the American occupational structure. Using 1973 data provided by the Census Bureau, Hauser and Featherman were once again able to chart occupational changes across generations of American men. They found that upward mobility continued to be high (in 1973, 49 percent were upwardly mobile and 19 percent were downwardly mobile, almost precisely the same as the 1962 figures); that the mobility table for black men was more like that of all men than it had been a decade earlier; that the length of schooling had an increasingly powerful effect on a man's occupational standing; that occupational returns to schooling were increasing, especially among blacks; that blacks had gained significantly in occupational status since 1962; and that 60 percent of this gain was explained by the higher levels of schooling attained by blacks by 1973.[21]

Assessing the implications of these findings, Featherman holds, first, that

the family and the school both are important sources of the socioeconomic achievements of men (and women) in modern America. Families provide cultural, intellectual, social and economic resources for achievement. The schools refine these resources and convert them into marketable skills and knowledge. But of the two, schooling is the greater source of variation in socioeconomic achievement, since one of the ways that the family and social origins in general affect achievement is through the schools. . . . [Second] a large component of the occupational achievement of men has nothing to do with social background or schooling. Success is not guaranteed by education, and humble origins do not preclude it. The third implication is that schooling is today an effective mechanism by which individuals can augment their stations in life and improve their standing relative to their own socioeconomic origins.[22]

The school performs two complementary functions, according to Featherman. On one hand, it reproduces the class system from generation to generation, since students from high-status families stay in school longer and thereby get high-status jobs. But its second function, which is far stronger and more effective than the first, is to sponsor the advancement of the most able regardless of their social origins. Citing William H. Sewell's longitudinal studies of 10,000 high school students in Wisconsin, Featherman notes that Sewell found "only 18 percent of all the educational differences in his sample to be associated with social class factors per se." Based on these and other studies, Featherman concludes that "it is impossible to support the claim that the process of schooling in modern America inherently and consistently reproduces the social class system."[23]

Hauser and Featherman's research shows that there is still a sizable gap between white and black occupational achievement, but it also reveals that there has been a significant narrowing of this gap during the past decade. It is important to recognize, as sociologist Seymour Martin Lipset has observed, that the considerable advances of younger and better educated blacks "did not happen as a result of the natural operation of sociological and economic factors, as had occurred earlier with various white ethnic groups. In the case of blacks, discrimination had to be countered by political forces." Political action by executive agencies, the Congress, the judiciary, and civil rights organizations was not ineffective, nor has liberal social policy been "decisively discredited," as Bowles and Gintis charge. It is indisputable that full equality has not been achieved, but equally indisputable in the light of the evidence is the conclusion that a democratic society can bring about effective social change, if there are both the leadership and the political commitment to do so. To argue, against the evidence, that meaningful change is not possible is to sap the political will that is necessary to effect change.[24]

CHAPTER SEVEN

A Critique of Radical Criticism

THE first major radical revisionist work, Michael Katz's *The Irony of Early School Reform*, was published in 1968. It has been the most influential, in part because it broke new ground by introducing the radical perspective to educational history, but also because it is a well written, sophisticated effort to apply social science concepts to historical problems. Because of its originality and its impact on subsequent scholarship, it has been one of the most significant books in its field during the past decade.

The central theme of *The Irony of Early School Reform* is Katz's interpretation of the reasons for educational reforms in the nineteenth century; they were not, he writes a "potpourri of democracy, rationalism, and humanitarianism. They were the attempt of a coalition of the social leaders, status-anxious parents, and status-hungry educators to impose educational innovation, each for their own reasons, upon a reluctant community." He argues that the irony of mid-nineteenth-century school reform is that it was not the product of working-class demands, but rather that it was imposed on an unwilling and skeptical working-class community by zealous social leaders. Consequently the working class became estranged from the school, which was perceived as an alien institution, and this estrangement "has persisted to become one of the greatest challenges to reformers of our own time."[1]

In a series of interrelated essays, Katz imaginatively explores the ramifications of educational reform and the ideology of educational reformers in nineteenth-century Massachusetts. He ranges easily across a wide field of disparate data, weaving facts and ideas into a coherent interpretation. He portrays reformers as middle-class and upper-class men with a clear sense of moral superiority and little hesitation in imposing their values on others. He suggests, too, their confusion and ambivalence as they tried to sort out the causes and effects of crime, vice, and poverty. A typically valuable insight is his observation that reformers advocated high schools both to promote industrialization and to cure its evil effects; by their activity, they contributed to the disintegration of the sense of community that they so vehemently espoused. His essay on the assumptions that led to the establishment of a state reform school for juvenile delinquents is a creative work of scholarship.

Frequently, his insights are more powerful than his analyses. When he examines the sources of professionalization, for example, his description of what happened is far more compelling than his explanations of why it happened. As educators became self-consciously professional, he holds, they turned inward and built a narrow world of their own; shielded by their self-righteous, salvationist, reformist rhetoric, they lost the capacity either to accept criticism or to criticize themselves. In explaining why he thinks this happened, he reconstructs a conflict between "soft-line" educators and "hard-line" educators. The soft-liners were reformers who believed in the importance of environment over heredity and in teaching through an appeal to the child's interest rather than obedience to authority; they "stressed the very qualities most necessary for social mobility and economic success," which meant self-discipline, inner motivation, and a refusal to accept the status quo as necessary. The hard-line educators held a Calvinistic, pessimistic, and conservative approach to such problems as crime, insanity, and education; they believed that man's inherent nature limited the possibility of change. The soft-liners considered the hard-liners to be harsh, authoritarian, and inflexible. Katz contends that the decisive victory of the soft-line over the hard-line "was a major defeat for the quality of American education," because it "marked the ending of serious educational debate." The soft-liners' triumph, he holds, was the result of an "almost brutal exercise of power" by Horace Mann and his allies.[2]

Katz's explanation raises more questions than it answers, largely because of his inadequate concern with the political process, the means by which educational policy decisions were made and changed. Why were the advocates of the hard-line unable to resurrect their views by appealing to the electorate, the community at large? Why were spokesmen for the hard-line unable to turn supporters of the soft-line in the state legislature out of office? Katz does not inform his readers whether they tried to do so. Mann's soft-line supporters in Boston ran for the school committee and got elected (Katz characterizes their election as "a takeover"); he notes that the soft-liners were not a majority on the school committee, and it is not clear why "their impact was strong," strong enough to cause a purge of the hard-line, conservative schoolmasters. Nor is it evident from Katz's account how the "brutal and vindictive" tactics of soft-line reformers in Massachusetts could account for the erosion of the hard-line in American education generally.[3]

Somewhat contradictorily, Katz states at the end of *The Irony of Early School Reform* that the hard-line, expressed as a belief in the importance of heredity over environment, has reappeared at the end of each soft-line, reform cycle. But is this apparently cyclical alternation of hard-line (hereditarian) and soft-line (environmentalist) ideology a "serious educational debate"? Should the articulation of both views be encouraged for the sake of a good debate and would such a debate improve the quality of American education? Apparently not, for he concludes that the hard-line should be seen as a threat to reform aspirations, a "rationalization for failure, an excuse for some relaxation of effort," thus allying himself with the soft-line reformers whom he has criticized throughout the book.[4]

The first portion of *The Irony of Early School Reform* is devoted to the analysis of a vote cast in Beverly, Massachusetts, in 1860, in which the townspeople abolished their two-year-old high school. The Beverly case is the most significant section of the book because it supplies the evidence for Katz's belief in "reform by imposition." Katz studied voter lists and tax rolls and concluded that the wealthy and the middle class supported the high school, while the working class voted against it. He holds that the promoters of the high school knew that the poor could not afford to dispense with their children's earnings and that they intended to spread "throughout the whole community the burden of educating a small minority of its children." The workers, he speculates, perceived the high school as a symbol of the industrialization that was destroying their independence and reducing their status; a vote against the high school was a vote against the advocates of industrial and economic development. He points out that the heaviest vote against the high school came from shoemakers, who at that very time were on strike because of a cut in their wages.[5]

The trouble with Katz's basic argument is that it violates the principle of Occam's razor: It suggests a complicated, inferential explanation where a far simpler one is sufficient to the data. As Katz notes, 56 percent of all those who voted against the high school had no school-age children, which was reason enough to object to a school tax. In addition, a majority of the opponents lived in sparsely populated, outlying districts, farthest from the high school. Either of these facts would explain the vote to abolish the school, as an expression of the nay-voters' self-interest.

Nor is Katz's interpretation strongly supported by his data. The commitment of the wealthy and the middle class to the high school is not as pronounced in his tabulations as it is in the body of the text. He writes that "a significant majority" of Beverly's "businessmen" supported the high school. Actually, the businessmen were almost evenly divided, with 30 in favor and 28 against the school. Of the 30 in favor, 4 were "business employees," who were probably clerks. If their vote is subtracted (because they were workers rather than businessmen), then the business vote was *against* the high school, 28 to 26, and a key element in Katz's argument is reversed. This weakness is even more evident in comparing the votes cast by "proprietors of business," who were 4 to 1 *against* the high school, to the votes of the "business employees," who favored the high school 4 to 0. These small numbers certainly have no statistical significance so far as American educational history is concerned, but within the scope of Katz's book they do not support the argument he founds on them.[6]

The shoemakers, who were then on strike, voted heavily against the high school, 80 to 29. Katz interprets their vote as "an opportunity to vent their anger in a perfectly legal way." But, oddly, his appendix reveals that their employers, the shoe manufacturers, *also* voted to abolish the high school, by a vote of 9 to 5. What seems as likely an explanation as Katz's is that the shoemakers were economically depressed by their recent cut in wages, as well as by loss of income during the strike, and were voting to reduce their taxes.[7]

Katz's opinion that school reform was exploitative is not fully sustained by his evidence. Neither the well-to-do nor the working class was monolithic in its vote. By finding that the high school was favored more by the well-to-do than by the workers, Katz proves the obvious: that the higher a family is on the socioeconomic scale, the more it values education, the more it will spend on its children's education, and the longer its children will stay in school.

He interprets this as an effort by the privileged to educate their children at the expense of the entire community, but nearly half of those who supported the high school did not have school-age children. Besides, his implication that tax funds should be spent only on services used by each segment of the community in proportion to its number is a narrow and regressive concept of public welfare; on that theory, government should not support public housing, public universities, public hospitals, public libraries, or any other good consumed disproportionately by any one segment of the community. Additionally, his view assumes that the poor and the working class are entitled to act on their self-interest, but that the well-to-do and the middle class are not.

Katz's historiographical argument is a debate with a straw man. "Older historians," he writes, identified "two distinct clusters of antagonists . . . : prominent, prestigious leaders and a working class. But the antagonists' attitudes defined by older historians must be reversed: the Beverly experience reveals that one dynamic of educational controversy was the attempt of social leaders to impose innovation upon a reluctant working class." His representation of the standard historiographical interpretation is not entirely accurate. Excepting Alice Felt Tyler, the standard works portray the advocates of schooling as a coalition of diverse social and economic groups, each with its own interests. Even Cubberley had a list of public school proponents that included not only "the intelligent workingmen in the cities," but seven other categories, such as " 'Citizens of the Republic'," "philanthropists and humanitarians," "public men of large vision," and "city residents." Cremin noted that both liberals and conservatives converged on the idea of a common school, for different reasons. Sidney Jackson and Merle Curti stressed the contradictory appeal of the public school both to those who wanted to maintain the status quo and to those who hoped to change it. This notion that the public school was extended by a coalition of disparate elements is actually sustained by Katz's data on Beverly, where nearly 25 percent of the vote for the high school came from workers, while another 28 percent came from men who were neither social leaders nor promoters of industrialism.[8]

What is missing in Katz's Beverly account is an appraisal of the politics of the town and the way in which it interacted with the politics of the school. We learn little of the political struggle that must have accompanied the establishment of the high school in 1858. We are told that there was an annual town meeting, but we do not learn how the town was governed or whether the anti-school majority controlled the political structure. Katz holds that "on the local level partisan politics was simply irrelevant" to educational reform, but he does not provide enough specific information to substantiate his judgment. There is no mention of whether the imminent Civil War had any bearing on the town's willingness to support a high school. It would have been interesting to know which citizens stayed silent when the high school's fate was voted on (were the abstainers workers, businessmen, or social leaders?). While Katz carefully details the history and social background of leading high school promoters, Joseph Thissell, who introduced the motion to abolish the high school, is never further identified. The reader quite naturally wonders what happened after the vote to disestablish the high school, how the community reacted, when a high school was reestablished, whether a new vote was taken, and which social groups supported or opposed the high school when it was re-created.[9]

In the concluding sentences of *The Irony of Early School Reform*, Katz writes:

We must face the painful fact that this country has never, on any large scale, known vital urban schools, ones which embrace and are embraced by the mass of the community, which formulate their goals in terms of the joy of the individual instead of the fear of social dynamite or the imperatives of economic growth. We must realize that we have no models; truly to reform we must conceive and build anew.[10]

The dilemma in Katz's formulation is his assumption that "the mass of the community" wants schools that stress "the joy of the individual" rather than discipline or economic betterment. Throughout the book, as well as in most of *Class, Bureaucracy, and Schools,* he assumes that the goals of educational radicals and working-class parents are the same. Only in the last chapter of the latter book does he acknowledge that the goals of the two groups may be quite dissimilar. He recounts a story of how educational radicals worked to elect a poor mother to a city school board without knowing her opinions on school issues; much to the radicals' surprise, they learned toward the end of the campaign that their candidate favored report cards and corporal punishment and opposed sex education. Katz reflected:

I suspect that what the poor want for their children is affluence, status, and a house in the suburbs rather than community, a guitar, and soul. They may prefer schools that teach their children to read and write and cipher rather than to feel and to be. If this is the case, then an uncomfortable piece of reality must be confronted: Educational radicalism is itself a species of class activity. It reflects an attempt at cultural imposition fully as much as the traditional educational emphasis on competition, restraint, and orderliness, whose bourgeois bias radicals are quick to excoriate.[11]

But this is an extraordinary reversal of the thrust of both of Katz's books. If the working class and the poor want their children to have a traditional education, to learn self-discipline, and to gain economic benefits from schooling, then their goals are not very different from those of the liberal, middle-class reformers of the nineteenth and early twentieth centuries. If this is so, then the "estrangement" between the working class and the school is either nonexistent or occurs only as the school abandons its "bourgeois" direction.

This is a profound dilemma, and few of the other radicals even consider it. Most take it for granted that "the people" want what educational radicals want for them, that participatory democracy in school policy will lead to joyful schools or even to the disestablishment of formal schools. The irony, perhaps, is that participatory democracy may facilitate the restoration of educational policies that radicals (and liberals) consider repressive and inhumane.

Politically, Katz's version of the radical analysis is curiously anti-activist, because of its characterization of reform as coercive social control. This radical critique, with its suspiciousness of reformers and of state action generally (since state action involves one small group of people—those in power—making laws for others—those not in power), is entirely consistent with an anarchistic outlook, but it implies a reactionary approach to social policy. Anyone who wants to better society is advised by this ideology to sit back and wait for indigenous change; Katz suggests that educational change might have been more successful if it had been "more slowly paced," if it had "come through community action," rather than having been imposed by impatient reformers. This perspective offers no support to those who "imposed" reform on rigidly segregated Southern communities nor to any other effort to change popular, but unjust, practices. If Katz is taken seriously, then the policymaker should certainly not risk becoming an overzealous reformer, forcing his views against the will of the majority. This position, based on the overriding value of participatory democracy, puts the educational radical at odds with the mainstream of liberalism, which makes heroes of dissenters, crusaders, and reformers, especially those who are willing to become, like Ibsen's Dr. Stockmann, "an enemy of the people." And it creates no way to deal with those situations where the will of the community is unjust and exploitative.[12]

The frontal attack on the liberal tradition is exemplified in *Roots of Crisis: American Education in the Twentieth Century,* a collection of essays by Clarence J. Karier, Paul Violas, and Joel Spring. The authors stress that their version of history is directly opposed to that of liberal historians like Merle Curti, Henry Steele Commager, Richard Hofstadter, and Lawrence A. Cremin, whom they categorize as apologists for the military-industrial, corporate-liberal state. The liberal historians are described as pragmatic humanitarians who believe in progress, social meliorism, and the "intelligent use of science and technology" to achieve a better life for mankind. Most people would consider that a flattering description, but the authors of these essays contend that the optimism of the liberals made them incapable of seeing "that this society is in fact racist, fundamentally materialistic, and institutionally structured to protect vested interests" and that the school "was in fact a vehicle of control and repression."[13]

The authors' conception of how history is written defines their methodology. As they explain in their introduction, how one interprets history is a function of how one views the present, and history is merely an extension of the historian's ideology. Their essays demonstrate repeatedly the dangers of a moralistic, presentist approach in which the authors scour the past for events and quotes to buttress their political views. Since the authors believe that all "facts" are conditioned by one's value judgments, they have free rein to argue polemically, with scant concern for questions of significance and context. Jane Addams is judged not by what she did but by a present-minded analysis of what she wrote; John Dewey is judged by isolated quotations from his writings, with little effort to demonstrate whether the offending essay or paragraph or sentence was representative of his thought or how it actually affected educational and social policy.[14]

Most of the essays in *Roots of Crisis* focus on the leading figures and trends of the progressive era, when the school was transformed into the primary agency of "social control." Cremin had seen the progressive thrust in education "as part of a vast humanitarian effort to apply the promise of American life," but Karier, Violas, and Spring see it as the rationalization of a coercive, repressive "corporate liberal state." Not humanistic concern, but testing, sorting, racism, and social stratification were the essential elements in progressive reform, according to the authors of *Roots of Crisis*. As Carl F. Kaestle has observed, a problem in analyzing "progressive education, if the phrase is taken to mean all educational innovation from 1890 through the 1920s, is the bewildering variety of programs and philosophies. The liberating, conformist, individualizing, and bureaucratizing tendencies set loose in these years make almost any interpretation possible if you look at the right group of people and statements."[15]

Instead of trying to evoke a sense of this "bewildering variety," of people working at cross-purposes, of arguments and uncertainty over ends and means, Karier, Violas, and Spring reduce the era to a monochrome, in which the leading figures are relentlessly bent on achieving control, stability, order, and efficiency. The generous and warm impulses that others have attributed to settlement-house workers and social reformers are denied and in their stead is seen only the desire to repress and homogenize any source of dissidence in the society. Those who seemed to be helping the needy were only pacifying them and neutralizing their discontent. In the radical perspective, the dominant impulse of the progressive period was not to improve schools and society, but to preserve social order while processing workers for industry. What once seemed remarkably complex becomes remarkably simple, as progressives and their contemporary opponents are melded into a single body of opinion with a complementary, coercive program and ideology.

The arguments advanced in these essays are for the most part too one-sided to deal adequately with the issues that are raised. The authors fail to probe the interrelationships among the various political and social movements of the progressive period. It was, after all, a period of enthusiasms, which included not only school reform, but such diverse causes as municipal beautification, prohibition, women's suffrage, eugenics, and immigration restriction. Were all of these different expressions of the same desire to perfect American society? Did they reach different audiences? Did their leaders argue with one another? How did radicals and progressives perceive one another? As with other complicated historical problems, the consideration of the cross-currents of the progressive era requires an open mind and an appreciation for subtlety and nuance.

Clarence J. Karier portrays liberals like Jane Addams and John Dewey as manipulative, middle-class builders of a "compulsory state," in which "nonviolent but coercive means" would be used to shape and control people; these "state-welfare" liberals aimed to Americanize immigrants, who were potential threats to the social order. Karier's chief target is John Dewey, whom he sees as a pillar of the establishment and a salesman of the emerging corporate order. He claims that Dewey was an assimilationist who "viewed ethnic and religious differences as a threat to the survival of society." Karier's major evidence for this charge is a confidential report on conditions among Polish-Americans that Dewey submitted to the federal government in 1918. Karier considers the report to be proof that Dewey "was mainly concerned with the manipulation of Polish affairs so that we would not lose our cheap immigrant labor supply after the war." Walter Feinberg, in his book *Reason and Rhetoric*, discusses this same study at length as evidence that Dewey was identified with "American military and commercial interests" and was undemocratically committed to assimilating the Polish.[16]

Karier's and Feinberg's interpretations of Dewey's Polish study have been challenged by Charles L. Zerby, who contends that they did not understand the historical situation in which the report was prepared. Zerby describes a factional struggle within the Polish-American community over the direction of postwar American policy towards Poland. One faction, which was composed of anti-Semitic, conservative monarchists, had achieved considerable access to the Wilson administration; the other, largely radicals and socialists, had not been able to make its case in Washington. Dewey's report urged the federal government to give the excluded faction a fair hearing. Ignoring Dewey's plea, the Wilson administration gave official recognition to the conservative group. Seen in this political context, the Polish report was not a refutation of Dewey's democratic principles, but a reaffirmation of those principles. Similarly, J. Christopher Eisele has maintained that the radical interpretation of Dewey's views on immigrants and assimilation has been "inaccurate and misleading; that Dewey was not attempting to homogenize ethnic differences or destroy ethnic culture; to the contrary, he favored the preservation of cultural differences and ethnic variables." Like Zerby, Eisele finds that the attack on Dewey has been pieced together from isolated quotations, divorced from their historical context. Eisele notes that Dewey, in a characteristic statement that is consistent with his actions and his writings, described the American concept of pluralism as "a complete separation of nationality from citizenship. Not only have we separated language, cultural traditions, all that is called a race, from the state—that is, from problems of political organization and power. To us language, literature, creed, group ways, national culture, are social rather than political, human rather than national, interests."[17]

The risk in calling up the past to support a political point relevant to the present is that the historical materials may be shaken loose from their original context. An egregious example of tailoring quotes to fit the writer's ideology is Paul Violas's essay on Jane Addams. The words he quotes are hers, but in repeated instances, the context and meaning have been altered to match his point, not hers. His selections from her works are meant to demonstrate Violas's belief that Addams sacrificed individualism for the sake of a unified, organic society. Her overriding commitment to a "new ideal community," he claims, brought her to reject the ties of family, social class, ethnicity, and nationality. He writes: "The immigrant, for Jane Addams, presented a threat because his different ethnic background disrupted American cultural unity. The relative ease, however, with which he could be stripped of his cultural foundations and reduced to the simplest common elements of humanity enhanced his value as a building block for her new community."[18]

Probably nothing less than a synoptic presentation of Violas's selections, alongside Addams's actual prose in its full context, could reveal the extent to which he has distorted the spirit of her words. He says, for instance, that "She rejected the family as a primary object of loyalty. Filial loyalty was too narrow and selfish: 'Our democracy is making in-roads upon the family, the oldest of human institutions, and a claim is being advanced which in a

certain sense is larger than the family claim'." In its context, the meaning of her sentence is unrelated to Violas's
point. Addams, in *Democracy and Social Ethics*, was writing specifically about the dilemma of the educated woman
in 1902, torn between those who tell her that her *only* role
is to raise a family and her own desire to serve in some
social role outside the family. She wrote:

The collision of interests, each of which has a real moral
basis and a right to its own place in life, is bound to be more
or less tragic. It is the struggle between two claims, the destruction of either of which would bring ruin to the ethical life. . . .
The failure to recognize the social claim as legitimate causes
the trouble; the suspicion constantly remains that woman's
public efforts are merely selfish and captious, and are not
directed to the general good.

She urged that the two claims should be adjusted so that
"neither shall lose and both be ennobled." Rather than
urging the atomization of the individual and the destruction of the family, as Violas suggests, Addams was asserting
the right of women like herself to become actively engaged in the world, to participate in "that life which
surrounds and completes the individual and family life."[19]
The footnote in Violas's essay which is supposed to
document Addams's rejection of ethnic groups as a basis
of identity refers to a page on which there is no mention
of ethnicity; however, on the pages immediately following
are Addams's views about how the Russian immigrants'
idealism and insatiable desire for justice "might be
utilized to a modification of our general culture and point
of view, somewhat as the influence of the young Germans
who came to America in the early fifties, bringing with
them the hopes and aspirations embodied in the revolu-

tions of 1848, made a profound impression upon the social and political institutions of America." Her point seems to be the opposite of the one Violas attributes to her. The entire corpus of her work rebuts Violas's contention that she wanted to strip the immigrants of their ethnic and cultural identity. Throughout her written works, as well as her life work, she consistently encouraged the preservation of immigrant traditions. In *The Spirit of Youth and the City Streets,* she wrote enthusiastically about the beauty of the folkways of America's many minorities, which she described as "an enormous reserve of material for public recreation and street festival." In a typical passage, she wrote:

Were American cities really eager for municipal art, they would cherish as genuine beginnings the tarantella danced so interminably at Italian weddings; the primitive Greek pipe played throughout the summer nights; the Bohemian theatres crowded with eager Slavophiles; the Hungarian musicians strolling from street to street; the fervid oratory of the young Russian preaching social righteousness in the open square.

In *Newer Ideals of Peace,* she wrote:

In our refusal to face the situation, we have persistently ignored the political ideals of the Celtic, Germans, Latin, and Slavic immigrants who have successively come to us; and in our overwhelming ambition to remain Anglo-Saxon, we have fallen into the Anglo-Saxon temptation of governing all peoples by one standard. We have failed to work out a democratic government which should include the experiences and hopes of all the varied peoples among us.[20]

Violas claims that Addams "proposed to teach the worker that even when his situation was desperate, industrial conflict was not necessary." This is an extreme distortion of both what she wrote and what she meant. Addams expressed the wish that strikes could proceed without violence because she believed that violence turns public opinion against the workers. She wrote:

> If the element of battle, of mere self-seeking, could be eliminated from strikes, if they could remain a sheer uprising of the oppressed and underpaid to a self-conscious recognition of their condition, so unified, so irresistible as to sweep all the needy within its flood, we should have a tide rising, not to destruction, but to beneficence. Let us imagine the state of public feeling if there had been absolutely no act of violence traceable, directly or indirectly, to the union miners; if during the long months of the strike the great body of miners could have added the sanction of sustained conduct to their creed. Public sympathy would have led to an understanding of the need these miners were trying to meet, and the American nation itself might have been ready to ask for legislation concerning the minimum wage, and for protection to life and limb. . . . But because the element of warfare unhappily did exist, government got back to its old business of repression.

Clearly, it was not industrial conflict she opposed, but violence. She not only opposed violence on principle, but because she believed that it hurt the workers' cause. While her pacifism may have been naive, it was sincere and not just a tactic to disarm the proletariat.[21]

Perhaps Violas's most outrageous misrepresentation is his suggestion that Addams presaged fascism, that her "concept of social control through mass psychology carried inherent implications for manipulation of the masses." His evidence for this charge is drawn from an essay in *The Spirit of Youth and the City Streets* where she was arguing against the commercialization of pleasure and in favor of better provision for public recreation. In place of commercial theaters, where young people were passively entertained, she advocated public games, choral groups, folk dancing, and other joyful activities that involved active participation. Addams described the great appeal of baseball thus: "The enormous crowd of cheering men and boys are talkative, good-natured, full of the holiday spirit, and absolutely released from the grind of life. . . . Does not this contain a suggestion of the undoubted power of public recreation to bring together all classes of a community in the modern city unhappily so full of devices for keeping men apart?" She wrote approvingly of "the festival, the street procession, the band of marching musicians, orchestral music in public squares or parks, with the magic power they all possess to formulate the sense of companionship and solidarity." Reacting to these lines, Violas solemnly comments:

This echo of enormous crowds of cheering men, martial music, parades . . . the expression of emotions through symbols, and the fusion of individual voices into a collective expression of solidarity reverberates through the charred corridors of the twentieth century with deafening resonance. A resonance which, of course, Miss Addams could not have anticipated.[22]

This suggestion that Jane Addams's appeal for more parks, more gymnasia, more sports and games, and more street music was an expression of incipient totalitarianism is simply incredible.

Karier's *Shaping the American Educational State* is yet another sounding board for the radical critique. His selection of readings and his introductions to them are intended to support his thesis that American educators have been unremittingly racist and that the system they created was designed to protect "the vested interests of the favored classes." The essays have been chosen to make Karier's point, rather than to explore any of the issues in depth. As he surveys American educators and their debates, conservatives, liberals, progressives, and reactionaries merge —all are racists, all servants of power. This blurring of distinctions makes it possible for him to refer to Arthur Jensen and William Shockley as "liberals," without explanation.[23]

The two issues that concern him most are academic freedom and testing as examples of liberal failure. The usefulness of the book is diminished by its one-sided interpretations and by the biased selectivity of its evidence. For example, Karier's omission of John Dewey's *New Republic* articles on testing is striking. It is highly doubtful that they were unknown to Karier, because they appeared immediately after the six articles by Walter Lippmann which are included in the collection. The only conceivable reason for leaving them out is that they constitute a sharp refutation of many of the allegations Karier has made against Dewey, as well as his larger effort to define progressives as sophisticated bigots. Far more eloquently than Karier, Dewey criticized the mental-testing movement, arguing cogently that the tests might become the basis for social stratification and an educational caste system. To have included Dewey's penetrating critique of testing would have compelled Karier to deal with complexity, for he would have found himself agreeing with one of his chief targets.[24]

Another instance of the partisan, even shrill, tone of this volume is an essay by Russell Marks. Marks maintains that the Carnegie Corporation underwrote Gunnar Myrdal's *An American Dilemma* because of the foundation's long-standing interest in blacks as "a valuable source of unskilled labor" and "a potential source of skilled labor." He asserts that the foundation's interest in blacks stemmed from Andrew Carnegie's realization of "the importance of fully utilizing Black labor," though he finds it unnecessary to demonstrate how Carnegie influenced the decision to fund Myrdal's study some twenty years after Carnegie's death. Myrdal, writes Marks, was chosen by "big business" with the expectation that he would bring an environmental interpretation to his findings. Thus, Myrdal's report "tended to legitimize the social order," since it treated the "Negro problem" as a moral issue rather than as a problem of capitalistic exploitation. Liberals, businessmen, and others came to realize that they could achieve greater "social control and social efficiency" and at the same time turn blacks into skilled laborers and willing consumers if only discrimination were reduced. Marks concludes: "From this social milieu which gave priority to efficiency and productivity emerged the Brown decision." This interpretation of the origins of the Brown decision, with Myrdal, the Supreme Court, businessmen, the Carnegie Corporation, and the civil rights movement conspiring to free blacks in order to better repress them, supposedly shows that there was no real disagreement between conservatives and liberals. In sum, the dissension and controversy that preceded and followed the Brown decision were more apparent than real because the outcome served the interests of the capitalistic social order. Karier found Marks's tendentious account so persuasive that he incorporated it into his presentation of the nature-nurture issue.[25]

The Great School Legend by Colin Greer is an effort to popularize the radical attack on liberalism and the public schools. It is not difficult for Greer to establish that not everyone succeeded in school and that some ethnic groups performed better than others. Much of his case rests on early twentieth-century school surveys, which showed high rates of educational "retardation" for recent immigrants, especially Italians. Greer interprets this to mean that schools were *designed* to fail large numbers, particularly minority children: "The failure of many children has been, and still is, a learning experience precisely appropriate to the place assigned them and their families in the social order. They are being taught to fail and to accept their failure." But Greer, by accepting the surveys at face value, simply reinforces the cultural limitations of early school officials.[26]

John Walker Briggs, in his study of the Italian immigrant experience, has directly challenged Greer's conclusions about Italian school "failure." Briggs establishes that Greer, like early twentieth-century researchers, confuses overageness with failure. Briggs demonstrates, by matching pairs of Italian and non-Italian children in the same classes, that Italian children customarily started school later, did not fail any more often, and were likelier to have superior attendance records. Without having looked beyond the flawed original sources, Greer repeatedly asserts that the schools never promoted much mobility. Actually, he never seriously investigates whether or not there has been mobility, but instead sets forth his negative thesis in such sweeping, deterministic terms that it can neither be proved nor disproved. The school's mission, he holds, was "to prevent political, social, or economic upheaval," and every seeming reform was merely a calculated effort to defuse class antagonisms. The argument is circular: Nothing ever changes because every alleged change strengthens the system and is therefore no change at all. Such closed, inflexible reasoning offers no way to understand how educational policy is made and how it changes, nor does it provide an assessment of the reciprocal relationship between immigrants and schools.[27]

Reason and Rhetoric: The Intellectual Foundations of Twentieth Century Liberal Educational Policy by Walter Feinberg is another attack on liberalism and progressivism. His chief complaint is that liberals and progressives failed to perceive the "fundamental conflict" between "the requirements of justice and the needs of technology." Rejecting the ideal of equal opportunity as an unsuccessful effort to wed these two purposes, Feinberg argues instead for a Rawlsian concept of equality, based not on meritocratic grounds but on the principle of justice.[28]

Dewey comes in for a large share of Feinberg's criticism, and much of it is based on the presentist assumption that Dewey should have known then what Feinberg knows now. For example, Feinberg perceives social class bias in John and Evelyn Dewey's *Schools of To-Morrow*, but radicals who were Dewey's contemporaries saw it differently. *The Modern School Journal*, a publication of educational radicals in the early twentieth century, frequently recommended the book that Feinberg now calls "class biased."[29]

Feinberg believes that Dewey's pragmatism "prohibited

thinking of human values, including freedom, in anything but provisional terms." This, he maintains, made Dewey a willing practitioner of social engineering and manipulation. Feinberg cites the following quotation from an article in 1917 in which Dewey was chiding pacifists for relying entirely on pure conscience:

If at a critical juncture the moving force of events is always too much for conscience, the remedy is not to deplore the wickedness of those who manipulate events. Such a conscience is largely self-conceit. The remedy is to connect conscience with the forces that are moving in another direction. Then will conscience itself have compulsive power instead of being forever the martyred and the coerced.

Feinberg comments on this statement: "It is questionable whether Dewey would have any room for the moral prophet unless he were successful in developing a political movement behind him. Certainly this statement would allow little room for the pacifism of World War I." This is an odd ground on which to criticize Dewey. Obviously, he was not trying to silence moral prophets; on the contrary, he was urging pacifists to organize in order to have an impact on policy. From his statement, it is clear that Dewey was urging pacifists to get involved in political action, to connect conscience "with the forces that are moving in another direction." Dewey was suggesting that while it is good to have progressive ideals and hopes, it is even better to strive effectively for their realization. Believing in the value of political efficacy is no fault, but rather represents a correct understanding of how policy is made in a democratic society: through a combination of organization and tactics that affects public opinion.[30]

Feinberg blames liberal reformers for not achieving a

truly just and egalitarian society, since they were willing to settle for less than complete justice and equality. He chastises reformers for failing to anticipate all the consequences of their actions and for failing to think and write the things that now, in retrospect, seem obviously desirable. Progressives such as Dewey and George Counts, he complains, were too willing to accept and encourage the advance of the technological society. Feinberg does not agree with Katz's hands-off attitude towards educational and social development (*Reason and Rhetoric* includes a sound critique of aspects of Katz's ideology); he believes reformers should have been more radical and more assertive in directing social change.

Feinberg does not explain how Dewey or Counts might have convinced industrialists to diminish their commitment to technology. Nor does he attempt to demonstrate the impact of Dewey's or Counts' writings. If Dewey and Counts and other progressives failed to question the rapid advance of technology and failed to understand how it would eventually affect American society, it may be that they were dazzled by technology's promise to improve the quality of life for the masses of people, to eliminate starvation, and to cure disease. Perhaps it was easier to foresee technology's benefits than to predict its spiritual and physical toll. Doubtless the modernizing process would have gone forward even if Dewey and Counts had never lived, just as it has in societies that never had a progressive movement. It is questionable whether a thoroughly radicalized, thoroughly Marxist Dewey and Counts would have had much impact at all on a society that was unreceptive to radical thought. They were men who lived in their times, not in ours, and it is unfair and ahistorical to expect them to have known what now seems apparent. Had they been radical enough to please their present critics, they would not have been central enough to be the focus of study today.

Rush Welter has commented, in a review of Feinberg and Karier, on their absorption with intellectual abstractions and their lack of "any useful sense of the frailty of human hopes." Neither author, he writes, "displays a sense that fallibility is part of the human condition rather than evidence of capitalist bias—that the errors of judgment and opinion men may detect today are quite likely to have been invisible or insurmountable for an earlier generation. . . . Similarly, neither seems to be aware of confusion and inadequacy as endemic human experiences." Instead, they "simply presuppose the existence, or rather the possibility, of a society in which all of their truths are served simultaneously. They offer no empirical example of such a society, of course; to do so might involve them in practical comparisons that would call their theories into question." This, he says, is the "utopian theorizing" of "academics whose trade is spinning words and who are insulated by those words from direct contact with experience." It is unreasonable for a historian to expect men and women engaged in public life over a number of years never to err, always to know what should be done and how best to do it. Only those who feel quite certain themselves about the identity of the truth can expect it of others; historians above all should have a decent respect for the tentativeness of the truth and the unreliability of absolutists.[31]

In the lead essay in Feinberg and Henry Rosemont, Jr.'s *Work, Technology, and Education*, James D. Anderson criticizes "liberal historians" who have written about the establishment of black public schools in the South. He writes that "the traditional liberal view . . . sees the rise of black schooling as the result of a humanitarian victory by a group of elite reformers over a reactionary white majority." He accuses scholars such as Louis Harlan, Horace Mann Bond, and Henry Bullock of "serious historical distortion" for treating Northern philanthropists as "patron saints" and Southern school reformers as idealists. His own view is that "black schooling was calculated to restrain black people and socialize them into a new form of subjection," specifically to train them as an inexpensive and docile labor force for the industrialization of the South.[32]

Anderson misrepresents Harlan, Bond, and Bullock. Their work encompasses his views, but with a far more sophisticated sense of the complexity of causes and effects than Anderson offers. None of them has the naively optimistic perspective that Anderson attributes to them. The very title of Harlan's book—*Separate and Unequal: Public School Campaigns and Racism in the Southern Seaboard States, 1901–1915*—contradicts Anderson's contention. The racism of the public school campaigners, both Northerners and Southerners, is a central theme in Harlan's book. He describes a Southern leader of the public school campaign, North Carolina Governor Charles B. Aycock, as a representative of the "conservative wing of the White Supremacy movement. A tacit bargain with him underlay the whole educational movement and dictated its tactical methods. The philanthropists acquiesced in disfranchisement and Jim Crow laws and undertook to promote acquiescence in the North." Through page after page, Harlan relates how the Northern industrialists sold out the claims of the blacks to equal status, how they directed their vast funds to support industrial education for blacks, and how they tolerated the racism of their Southern associates.[33]

Bullock and Bond are similarly misrepresented by Anderson. Bullock specifically describes the economic motives of the Northern industrialists; one of them, writes Bullock, "went South as a businessman conscious of the value of Negro labor. He considered this labor necessary to the efficient operation of his railroad, for he needed thousands of Negro workers—but needed them trained." Bullock also documents the racism of the Northerners who promoted caste education for blacks. Bond, writing four decades earlier than Anderson, while Southern black schools were still at the mercy of white racists and still dependent on Northern philanthropy, was no Pollyanna; he criticized industrial education and its sponsors. But he did write appreciatively of the role that Northern philanthropy had played in stimulating public responsibility for black schools and in providing higher education for blacks. Writing in 1934, he viewed the philanthropic effort strictly within the political context of the alternatives. He believed that half a loaf, perhaps even just a slice, was better than nothing at all, and he strongly suspected that most Southern whites, if left to their own initiative, would have preferred no black schools.[34]

In addition to misstating the interpretations of "liberal historians," Anderson corrupts some of his original sources for the sake of his argument. He says that Edgar Gardner Murphy, a Southern school reformer, wrote that

black education, like slavery, was to serve as a system for restraint. Murphy viewed the purpose of black education as that of arresting the upward and downward momentum of blacks. The education of blacks was defined as dangerous if it allowed them to descend into industrial inefficiency. Black schooling was viewed as equally dangerous if it encouraged blacks to desire the same economic, social, and political status as whites. The function of schooling was to exercise restraint.

But Murphy was writing about slavery, not about black education. This is what he wrote:

Slavery was nothing if not a system of restraint. . . . This bondage fixed, instinctively, a limit beyond which the negro must not ascend; it fixed a limit below which the negro must not fall. It operated in both directions as a check. . . . Upon the two tendencies of the negro thus held in check, the effect of emancipation must be evident. Restraint withdrawn, negro life is released in two directions—the smaller number of better negroes is permitted to rise, and many of them do rise; the larger number of weaker negroes is permitted to fall, and most of them do fall.[35]

A somewhat comical example of slipshod research occurs when Anderson quotes a black bishop who told a Congressional committee that Southern blacks needed better educational opportunities. Anderson writes, "Holsey [sic] could certainly make such statements as he had made himself literate by studying graves in the woods during slavery." That might have been a remarkable way to become literate, but it is not the way that Bishop Halsey learned to read. According to his testimony, he bought a Webster's speller and dictionary and taught himself to read while still a slave. After Emancipation, he decided that he "would abandon everything and go into the woods and learn how to read and write properly." Each day for two years, he went into the woods with books on grammar, spelling, geography, writing, history, and theology. This is indeed an inspiring story of self-education. But where did Anderson get the idea that Bishop Halsey made himself literate "by studying graves in the woods"? From a boldface subtitle in the midst of Halsey's printed testimony, "Grave Studies in the Woods," in which "grave" is a synonym for "serious."[36]

Samuel Bowles and Herbert Gintis's *Schooling in Capitalist America: Educational Reform and the Contradictions of Economic Life* is a straightforward Marxist critique of American education and society. Their thesis is that the purpose of American schools is to reproduce the unequal social relations of production. Bowles and Gintis, who are economists, chide the radical historians for portraying educational development as the result of class domination rather than class conflict. The real function of the schools, they maintain, is to prepare youths for their adult roles in a hierarchical, undemocratic economic order, not to advance economic equality nor to encourage full human development. They attribute the failure of the radical school reform movement to its insufficient understanding of the subordination of the schools to the needs of the capitalist economy.

Their presentation of American educational history reflects their Marxist perspective. They emphasize whatever supports their thesis and ignore or explain away whatever doesn't. Events of the past are shown either to correspond to capitalist imperatives or to be contradictions generated by capitalism. School reforms that took root were a sham because they bolstered the capitalist system, and school reforms that failed were rejected because they threatened the capitalist system. The argument is not susceptible to disproof: The schools don't promote equality or personal liberation because the capitalist system won't let them, but when they do, it is in order to delude the people and serve capitalism. Both A and not-A are advanced as evidence for the same point.

Why is it, Bowles and Gintis ask, that family background continues to have as much influence over educational attainment as it did 30 years ago? Why is it that "the substantial equalization of educational attainments over the years has not led measurably to an equalization in income among individuals?" They contend that inequality is transmitted from generation to generation, not by superior genes or superior ability, but by the "structure of production and property relations" under capitalism. A major role of the educational system is "in hiding or justifying the exploitative nature of the U.S. economy." Specifically, the schools prepare youth for "the undemocratic and class-based character of economic life in the United States." Schools perpetuate the class structure by teaching students to accept relationships of dominance and subordinancy, fragmenting them into stratified status groups by race, sex, and social class, and preparing "reserve armies of skilled labor," all under the rubric of the "technocratic-meritocratic" ideology of equal opportunity.[37]

Bowles and Gintis's attitude toward the United States economic system is central to their analysis. As Marxists, they find it "highly dictatorial," "profoundly undemocratic," "autocratic," and "formally totalitarian," because "the actions of the vast majority (workers) are controlled by a small minority (owners and managers)." It is, furthermore, typified by the "hierarchical division of labor and bureaucratic authority" and systematically stratified by "race, sex, education, and social class." Hierarchy, bureaucracy, and social stratification are utilized by capitalists to stabilize this "totalitarian system of economic power." Since economic inequality and social injustice are systemic to capitalism, educational policy is an ineffective lever of change.[38]

The proliferation of corporations and bureaucracies has turned white-collar workers into a new proletariat, in their view, as alienated and powerless as assembly-line workers. The only historical analogies they can find for our present form of capitalist hierarchical control are "the Southern slave-plantation sector," and possibly the post-Civil War sharecropping and crop-lien systems. Not surprisingly, they find that capitalism is at the root of all our present problems: "Capitalism and the 'Anxious Society' are one. Drugs, suicide, mental instability, personal insecurity, predatory sexuality, depression, loneliness, bigotry, and hatred mark the perennial fears of Americans." The only appropriate response to this monstrous set of conditions is revolution, because the American economy is "the most extensive and complete wage-labor system in the history of civilization . . . repressive and anachronistic, an obstacle to further human progress."[39]

The authors call their revolution "socialist" and "democratic," but their referents are never socialist democracies like Sweden or Israel. Instead, they hail the revolutionary "socialism" of such nations as the Soviet Union, North Vietnam, Cuba, and China. And, while appealing to the antiauthoritarian sympathies of American radicals, they ultimately advise "socialist" educators to "reject simple antiauthoritarianism and spontaneity" as insufficiently revolutionary, "barren and naively individualistic."[40]

Bowles and Gintis are quite right that family background continues to influence educational attainment (a relationship well documented by American social science), though the power and the persistence of that relationship are not necessarily as certain as they indicate. As noted earlier, William H. Sewell has found that no more than 18 percent of the variance in educational attainment can be explained solely by socioeconomic background, and Hauser and Featherman have concluded that the relative importance of social background on educational attainment has apparently declined in recent years. In a free society, government can try to neutralize social differences by subsidizing tuition, but it cannot (or at least has not) actually penalize children from advantaged homes as a means of advancing equality. Thus, it is not surprising that educated parents are likelier to implant higher educational aspirations in their children and are more capable of paying for advanced education than are those parents who have little education and low income.[41]

What is surprising is that, according to recent sociological studies, the same phenomenon occurs in the Soviet Union. Despite official policies that are egalitarian, there is evidence that the best places in the best schools go disproportionately to children of the highest social strata. According to Mervyn Matthews, the competition for limited university places "raises the familiar problem of selection," and there is "a close relationship between a Soviet citizen's chances of getting into a VUZ* and his social background, very much as in other advanced countries. Children from richer, better educated, or more secure families find the task easier than their less favored con-

* A higher education institution.

temporaries." A number of recent studies by Soviet scholars confirm this pattern. A study in Gorky showed that the upper grades tended to be filled by children of the intelligentsia; another demonstrated that children of white-collar workers got better marks than those of manual workers. A comparison of the social background of applicants and students at Rostov University revealed that candidates from the intelligentsia were a quarter of the applicants but half of those accepted, while the proportion of peasants dropped from 15 percent to 2.5 percent. Indeed, "the Soviet pattern is quite similar to that which obtains in bourgeois countries, and seems to have shown a remarkable stability over several decades." The resurgence of similar patterns in China is likely, now that admission to universities will again be based on competitive examinations, rather than social origins (after the Cultural Revolution, children of peasants were favored, while children of the educated were discriminated against); the purpose of the change, which followed the ouster of "the gang of four," is not to reassert social inequality but to improve the quality of research and the pace of technological development in China.[42]

The thesis itself—that the purpose of schools is to reproduce and legitimate inequality—rests on inferences about the implicit functions of the schools. Bowles and Gintis carry to an extreme the sort of functionalist analysis that characterizes the work of the radical historians. Functionalist analysis, when applied thoughtfully and carefully, may lead to useful insights about the way institutions operate and about the differences between intention and behavior. But when used loosely, it is nothing more than speculation masquerading as sociology. It is well known to social scientists that children whose parents are well educated and economically secure are likely to stay in school longer and do better academically than children whose parents are poor and uneducated.

Does this mean, as Bowles and Gintis take it, that the *purpose* of the school is to lock the children into the status of their parents? Isn't it possible that the high achievement of one child and the low achievement of another may have other causes which preceded their schooling and whose effects are more persistent than that of schooling? If so, are they then confusing a correlation (between parental status and student performance) with a causal relationship (since poor kids do badly in school, the *function* of schools is to keep poor kids down)? How is one to test assertions about the needs of capitalism or the purposes of the "capitalist class"? The trouble with such sweeping claims is that they cannot be proved or disproved. How is one to know what the underlying function of schools really is? The Marxist, the anarchist, the liberal, the conservative, the churchman, the school official, the teacher, the parent, the student, etc.—each has his own view of what the underlying function of schooling *really* is. It should be obvious that any analysis that relies essentially on opinion rather than evidence is of largely hortatory value.

Bowles and Gintis buttress their argument for the economic irrelevance of education by contending that income inequality has remained constant since 1910 (though prominent economists like Arthur Okun and Simon Kuznets maintain that income inequality was significantly reduced during World War II). A different light was cast on this issue by economist Morton Paglin. Paglin holds that the usual concept of income equality fails to take into account the different income needs of families at different stages of the life cycle. He argues that perfect equality would mean "equal incomes for all families at the same stage of their life cycle, but not necessarily equal incomes between different age groups." Additionally, Paglin points out that the actual extent of inequality is exaggerated

by a statistical decision to exclude need-based in-kind transfers from the definition of income. As a matter of social policy, we have decided to mitigate poverty by making large transfers in the form of public housing, rent supplements, food stamps and food assistance, medicaid, and social services such as day care, etc. We then blithely exclude these transfers from the statistics on poverty and inequality and wonder about the lack of improvement in the share allotted to the lowest quintile!

After calculating readjustments for transfer payments and for the age composition of the population, Paglin concludes that inequality of income declined by 23 percent in the period from 1947 to 1972. Similarly, recalculations by the Congressional Budget Office in early 1977 showed that governmental social welfare programs had reduced the rate of poverty in the United States by sixty percent in the past decade. In 1965, there were 9.5 million families in poverty, or 15.8 percent of all families; by 1975, with transfer payments included, the number of families in poverty dropped to 5.4 million, or 6.9 percent of American families.[43]

The systematic understatement of the real impact of governmental programs during the decade after 1965 has been useful to strange bedfellows: to radicals, who believe that liberal reforms are doomed to ineffectiveness; to conservatives, who never wanted to spend the money in the first place; and to some shortsighted liberals, who believe that any evidence of success would slacken the national commitment to do something about poverty. But this continued refusal to acknowledge any degree of achievement and progress has had political consequences, for it has undercut political support for the very programs whose success has gone unacclaimed. This serves the purposes of radicals and conservatives, but it is a self-defeating strategy for liberals.

The way that Bowles and Gintis present the data on income inequality—in the form of a bar graph—accentuates the extent of inequality by referring only to percentage "shares" of the national income for each quintile without also providing absolute dollar figures. Their bar graph shows that the poorest quintile of families received 5.4 percent of total personal income in 1974, the second quintile 12.0 percent, the third quintile 17.6 percent, the fourth quintile 24.1 percent, and the richest quintile 41.0 percent (these percentages do not include corrections for transfer payments, as Paglin points out). When the percentages are translated into 1976 dollars, it turns out that the upper limit of income for the lowest quintile is $7,441; for the second quintile, $12,400; for the third quintile, $17,300; for the fourth quintile, $23,923; and the mean income for the top 5 percent of the income distribution is $37,047. Or, looked at another way, the mean income for each quintile from poorest to richest is: $4,555; $9,953; $14,845; $20,328; $34,688. There is clearly inequality of income, but the gap between quintiles and from bottom to top is not nearly so great as the percentages alone seem to suggest.[44]

One's credulity is ultimately strained by the gratuitous,

ideological asides that pepper the book. Thus, the authors explain mass immigration to the United States in the nineteenth century: "Millions of Europeans, many of them peasants driven out of business by cheap U.S. grain imports, came to the U.S. in search of a living wage." No recognition from this quarter for the United States as a haven from religious and political persecution! And there is the ironic contrast between the authors' contention that the capitalist class exercises its control over educational policy through its foundations and their own acknowledgment of a three-year grant from the Ford Foundation (are they then instruments of the capitalist class, bolstering the system by ineffectually attacking it?) .[45]

It is doubtful that capitalism is the independent variable in all of the social and political maladies described by Bowles and Gintis. Bureaucracy and hierarchical control are not unique to capitalist societies. If anything, these institutional forms are even more firmly entrenched in Marxist and socialist countries. And anyone acquainted with the societies lauded by the authors must feel some skepticism about the claims of greater personal freedom in Marxist "democracies."

To be sure, there are aspects of Bowles and Gintis's critique of American society that are worthy of attention. It is valuable and stimulating to perceive the totality of American education from a Marxist perspective, though one might wish that the authors showed some slight appreciation for the democratic-liberal values that preserve their freedom to publish a call to revolution against democratic liberalism. Unfortunately, even when they document their points with solid evidence, their analysis hews so uncritically to Marxist conventionalities that the overall impression is of a one-sided polemic, whose logic is reductionist and whose questions are raised with answers in hand.

One of the most perplexing dilemmas for radical critics is whether to stress liberty or equality as the most important end for society. Most of them simply ignore the tension between the two values and assume that it is possible to have a society and a kind of schooling where both liberty and equality are maximized, while bureaucracy and administrative system are minimized, if not eliminated altogether. That this is a chimera is apparent to Bowles and Gintis, who know that revolutionary egalitarianism cannot be achieved without extensive political and social controls. At the other extreme is Joel Spring, who is an anarchist concerned with individual liberty. It stands to reason that an egalitarian society must have a coercive governmental bureaucracy with the power to make people equal; similarly, Spring's opposition to the "existence of the state in any form" presupposes acceptance of extreme inequality. Degrees of liberty are purchased with degrees of equality, and vice versa. Spring is against all governments, whether communist or democratic: the former are openly autocratic, while the latter require the individual "to sacrifice his autonomy either to the majority or to a representative." As an anarchist, he rejects all institutions, whether school, church, or family, that try "to make the individual into something."[46]

Spring's *Education and the Rise of the Corporate State* relates the history of twentieth century American education from an anarchist perspective. The first sentence states his thesis: "The corporate image of society turned American schools into a central social institution for the production of men and women who conformed to the needs and expectations of a corporate and technocratic world." The public schools "were organized to meet the needs of the corporate state and consequently, to protect the interests of the ruling elite and the technological machine." The corporate state was the creature of businessmen, labor leaders, and progressive politicians. All combined to eliminate obsolete individualism and to spread the gospel of cooperation and social purpose.[47]

The major victory of progressivism, he believes, was to instill in teachers and pupils the importance of group endeavor and the value of dedication to the common good. The well-schooled child was a conformist, ready to sacrifice himself for the group. The specific mechanisms for downgrading individualism were: the removal of competition for grades and awards; group projects; efforts to meet the needs of children and their families with vacation schools, social centers, parks, playgrounds, and other recreational facilities; anti-urban activities like summer camps; extracurricular activities like clubs, athletics, assemblies, and student government. All of these seemingly beneficent or innocuous activities, writes Spring, "involved control of behavior through training and mental forms of persuasion. In a sense the American revolution replaced the use of force with education as a means of maintaining social order."[48]

Spring detects a compromise by the individual in any activity that is planned for the good of society. He criticizes guidance because it was "one form of education designed to make the economic system run efficiently for the benefit of all. But vocational guidance was only part of a general educational plan to turn society into one large corporation of brotherly love. Another part of the plan was the creation of a guaranteed annual income that would condition men to think in terms of working for the good of society." On this count, many twentieth-century liberals are guilty as charged, for they have consistently urged the consideration of the good of society, and in recent years, many have even advocated that American society would be better, more just, and more equal if there were something like a guaranteed annual income.[49]

In *A Primer of Libertarian Education*, Spring carries the anarchist analysis further. He holds that "a new society cannot be born unless a new person is born that can function within it." Spring agrees with Wilhelm Reich, who linked the "authoritarian character structure" to authoritarian child-rearing methods and sexual repression. To achieve freedom, Spring proposes the following: first, the elimination of the school, because it attempts to mold children "into some particular moral or social ideal"; second, the abolition of the nuclear family, which is responsible for perpetuating middle-class morality and denying freedom to women; third, the removal of adolescent restrictions: "at as early an age as possible the child must become a miniature adult, a person exercising all the rights and privileges that we now confer on adults." This last proposal would be accomplished by making children legally "free" at the age of twelve or thirteen and guaranteeing them a government income until the age of twenty-one. To assure adolescent sexual freedom, special residences would be set up (by government?) and birth control devices supplied. All of this would lead to a libertarian society, where children were free from repressive authority and assured of "genital freedom." Spring's utopia sounds remarkably like an adolescent fantasy: If only kids had money, sex, and freedom from being hassled by parents, then everything else in society would be okay.[50]

Much of the historical background in *A Primer of Libertarian Education* was first set out by Spring in *Education and the Rise of the Corporate State* and in his essay "Anarchism and Education: A Dissenting Tradition." The thrust of his historical research has been an attempt to create an anarchist tradition in education, one that is relevant to the present. While there is certainly a radical tradition of richness and depth, it remains questionable whether there is a usable anarchist past. Spring's case for an anarchist tradition is frequently based on adroit picking and choosing among his original sources—ignoring some arguments, emphasizing others, and when necessary, blending the activities of anarchists with those of non-anarchist radicals and nonradical progressives.

Spring cites William Godwin's argument against national systems of education in 1793 as an early expression of anarchism in education. Godwin feared that government might use its control of educational institutions to maintain itself in power and to stifle free inquiry. In a grotesque overstatement, Spring claims that Godwin was proven right because "Whether in Nazi Germany or in the United States, clearly the school by its very nature had become an institution for political control." In "its very nature," the school was "consciously designed to change and shape people" and was therefore a "weapon" in the service of whichever state controlled it. But this is a superficial analysis of the problem of the relationship between the state and the schools. What distinguishes totalitarian states is that they take over all institutions and communications media, not just the public schools; even artistic expression, which ought to be entirely free, came under strict regulation in Nazi Germany and the communist dictatorships. Having the benefit of history, Spring should be able to differentiate between the schools of Nazi Germany and those of the United States, in terms of the nature and purpose of their control, as well as the existence in the United States of discordant, independent, competing channels of education and information.[51]

An example of purposeful selection is Spring's treatment of the educational ideas of Francisco Ferrer, a radical Spanish educator who was executed as an insurrectionary in 1909. Very likely, his crime was his founding of the Modern School in Barcelona in 1901, a free-thinking institution that was directly, openly critical of the Spanish government, the Catholic Church, capitalism, and other conventional dogmas of the time.

Spring describes Ferrer as an anarchist educator who exemplifies Spring's belief that schools should not impose any particular goals on their pupils nor mold their character in any way. Ferrer, however, in his own writings presents a very different picture of his efforts. The Modern School was created not as an anarchist school, but as a "Modern, Scientific, and Rational School" (its original name). Ferrer opposed dogma, but he did not eschew character-forming activities. He believed that "a rational and scientific education would preserve children from error, inspire men with a love of good conduct, and reorganize society in accord with the demands of justice." Ferrer had his own values, as well as his own notion of what constituted "error," "good conduct," and "the demands of justice." Furthermore, the Modern School carried on what Ferrer called

a discreet and systematic campaign against [uncleanliness], showing the children how a dirty person or object inspires repugnance, and how cleanliness attracts esteem and sympathy; how one instinctively moves toward the cleanly person and away from the dirty and malodorous; and how we should be pleased to win the regard of those who see us and ashamed to excite their disgust.

Spring ignores the Modern School's hygiene program, which was a kind of socialization, though he quickly condemns similar efforts in American public schools as techniques of social control.[52]

Spring establishes artificial barriers between progressives and radicals in his rendering of early twentieth century history, and he persistently distorts and caricatures the progressive tradition. Progressives, he contends, were builders of the compulsory corporate state, while radicals and anarchists were critics of the repressive mainstream. His own evidence demonstrates that this is a false polarity, an untenable oversimplification of the swirling intellectual currents of the period. He does not acknowledge the extent to which ideas and personalities crossed ideological and political lines during the progressive era. He claims the work of George Counts and Scott Nearing as part of the radical tradition, but they were also part of the progressive movement. Dewey was a progressive, but he frequently allied himself with radicals and anarchists on particular issues, and they in turn frequently borrowed his ideas.

Spring's admiring treatment of the Modern School at Stelton, New Jersey, reveals the limitations of his approach. He cites the school as an example of a successful libertarian school but fails to acknowledge its debt to progressive educational concepts. Having declared himself an advocate of the radical-anarchist-libertarian tradition, he ascribes whatever is good in the school to its radical heritage, but overlooks practices and ideas that he would criticize in public institutions. For instance, while he detects "romantic pastoralism" and "anti-urban feeling" in public school officials who take city children to the country or encourage nature study, he sees nothing of the kind when radicals open boarding schools for workers' children in rural settings, such as the Manumit School in Pawling, New York, "located on a 177-acre farm with cattle, hills, and a stream for swimming and fishing," or the Modern School at Stelton, established (in the words of its founders) on 68 acres "out in God's open country," far from the conventionalities and shams of city life."[53]

The Modern School was founded in 1913 not only by anarchists and radicals, but by socialists, single-taxers, free-thinkers, and labor unionists; significantly, its list of supporters included the Progressive Education Association. In its first decade, the school went through a succession of teachers, each with his or her own understanding of libertarian education. But despite the turnover of teachers, there was a consistency of approach that reflected the ferment within progressive circles. The emphasis was on getting away from abstract academic studies and moving toward a program of active learning, or "self-activity." One teacher called it "Heart, Hand, and Head." Others, like Alexis and Elizabeth Ferm, who directed the school for many years, favored manual training, handicrafts, the arts, workshops, and other nonabstract kinds of learning. It is clear as one reads accounts of the Modern School that while its supporters' politics were more radical than that of progressives, their educational approaches were indebted to many of the same sources.[54]

Spring's programmatic suggestions at the conclusion of *A Primer of Libertarian Education* raise important questions about the nature of freedom. How far can an anarchist go in imposing his views on others and still remain an anarchist? He never explains why it is any less coercive to socialize children to anarchism than to socialize them to some other ideal of the good life. What he offers is compulsory libertarianism, legislative enactments to destroy the nuclear family and other traditional institutions. Those parents who want to educate their children traditionally would find the power of the compulsory libertarian state arrayed against them. It is a curious contrast with our present, much maligned society, where anarchists and libertarians are free to reject compulsory marriage, free to avoid public schools, and free to raise their children as they please. Those who agree with Spring have far greater personal choice at present than would those who disagree with him in his projected new society. In his libertarian utopia, the individual would be "freed" from his roots, his culture, his family, his history, and ultimately, the confines of his own identity. It is a prescription for the fully anomic society.

After *A Primer of Libertarian Education*, Spring published *The Sorting Machine: National Educational Policy since 1945*. While maintaining his libertarian perspective, Spring avoids the excessive politicization and romantic distortions of his earlier works and connects to reality in a way that they fail to do. Without resort to polemical bravura, he questions whether Americans' emphasis on schooling as a mechanism of social reform and economic development has unnecessarily compromised concern for individual development. This point, which was also made in Rita Kramer's biography of Maria Montessori to explain the rejection of her individualistic methods by progressive educators, deserves further serious consideration. *The Sorting Machine* suggests the possibility that the radical-anarchist orientation, when grounded in a realistic appraisal of American politics and disciplined by historical craftsmanship, might make important contributions to our understanding of educational policy.[55]

CHAPTER EIGHT

A Summing Up:
Limitations of the
Ideological Approach

EDUCATIONAL history, whether written by intellectual historians, social historians, or economic historians, offers broad vistas for new and significant research into human behavior, social processes, and political decision-making. The issues are complicated, and they go directly to the core of American life and thought. Freed of the Cubberleyan tradition, educational historians are studying, among other things, family and community life, the communications media, religion, race, ethnicity, and group biography. With a perspective informed by the social sciences, historians are using new techniques to reinvestigate old issues and ask new questions. The school is seen as one of a number of educating institutions that influenced the lives of Americans. While this conception of education may seem to derogate the role of the school, it does more nearly approximate the educative experiences of most Americans.

In light of these trends, it becomes increasingly difficult to write about the school historically without setting it within a wide social context. But it is one thing to assess the political, economic, and social functions of the school and quite another to "discover" these functions as though they were clandestine purposes, hidden until now by capitalist conspirators. The difference in emphasis is the difference between a political analysis of history and a politicization of history. The former seeks to understand causes and effects in their historical context, the latter imposes a particular interpretation on past events.

Politicization has many risks, the greatest of which is that it frequently forces a telescoping and distortion of the past for the sake of explaining the present. The presentist method involves projecting one's own ideas onto the past in search of the seeds of present problems. The more passionate the seeker, the likelier he is to treat the past as a precursor of the great goodness or great evil of the present, rather than on its own terms. While present-day problems obviously have their origins in the past, the historical inquiry must be informed by a respect for the importance of context. Nothing that exists today has precisely the same meaning that it had a century ago; the perceptions of the 1970s are not the same as those of other eras.

As David Hackett Fischer has pointed out, the impulse to use history for political purposes is not new; it has been indulged in by scholars of all political persuasions, by communists and anti-communists, by conservatives and liberals, and most recently, by young radical historians, who

regard all aspirations to objectivity as a sham and a humbug, and stubbornly insist that the real question is not whether historians can be objective, but which cause they will be subjective to. . . . To make historiography into a vehicle for propaganda is simply to destroy it. . . . The fact that earlier generations and other ideological groups have committed the same wrong does not convert it into a right.[1]

The presentist orientation of the radical historians is freely acknowledged. The authors of *Roots of Crisis* aver that

If one starts with the assumption that this society is in fact racist, fundamentally materialistic, and institutionally structured to protect vested interests, the past takes on vastly different meanings. The authors of these essays write from such a conception of the present, which shapes our own view of the past.

Katz, defending the manifest presentism of *Class, Bureaucracy, and Schools,* states that "Our concerns shape the questions that we ask and, as a consequence, determine what we select from the virtually unlimited supply of 'facts'." The conviction that American public schools are inherently racist, pathologically bureaucratic, and class-biased informs the radicals' decision to read the past into the present and the present into the past. Their stated intention is to spur radical change in the schools and the larger society, but the effect of their arguments is quite different. If policymakers heed Katz, they will resist taking initiatives and "imposing" reforms on the people; judges too would be restrained from forcing educational change upon reluctant communities. If they heed Karier, they will abandon any effort to work within a system that is fundamentally "racist and designed to protect class interest." If they heed Bowles and Gintis, they will see the futility of any educational reform within a capitalist society. If they heed Spring, they will cease being policymakers altogether. As Sol Cohen has observed, "The ideological commitment of the radical revisionists, far from being a road to action, has become a dead end." If reformers in the past have been power-hungry, manipulative, and devious, why trust reformers in the present? If past reforms have served hidden "vested interests" rather than the people, why assume beneficial consequences from present reforms? If class connections are so compelling, what are we to make of the radical revisionists themselves, all of whom are, by professional status and income, members of the same upper middle-class group that has traditionally led reform movements?[2]

Educational history is a particularly tempting arena for politicization because of the ready availability of the public school as a straw man, a panacea that failed. School officials and reformers spoke glowingly of the Great American Public School, the Bulwark of Democracy, that was supposed to make everyone equal and happy and successful. As more people stayed in school longer, society was supposed to become better and wiser. But clearly everyone is not equal and happy and successful, nor have inequality, injustice, war, and corruption vanished with the extension of schooling. Therefore, say the politicized historians, the people who sold us on schooling deceived us; the schools were a fraud from the beginning and intentionally so.

But this is a simplistic rendering of the past. There have

been at least two traditions of education commentary that exist side by side. One lauds the greatness of the public school, the other laments its lowly state. The first was the creation of promoters and local officials, waging intensive campaigns for public funds and stressing the accomplishments of the schools. The other was what Richard Hofstadter called "the educational jeremiad" of reformers and critics. The two traditions interacted, for the propagandists knew that the American public had to be convinced of the value of schooling, in terms of their own interest. No one in the nineteenth or early twentieth century was taken in by rhetoric alone, particularly when it contradicted one's own experience. There were plenty of people who had gotten ahead without much schooling. The Horatio Alger rags-to-riches stories were not testimonials to the schools, but to the rewards of hard work, good character, and luck. As Hofstadter showed, Americans have had an anti-intellectual strain that precluded any automatic respect for credentials; typically, schooling was appreciated for its cash value, not as an engine of social reconstruction. Schoolmen, addressing a skeptical public that held the purse strings, alternately spoke rhapsodically and despairingly of the schools that might be and the schools that were.[3]

From this mixed bag of hope, despair, promise, and complaint, and from a motley company of idealists, pragmatists, cynics, and moralists, the politicized historians select the passages and the quotes that make their case against American schooling and the liberal tradition. A history that is rich with controversy and complexity is reduced to a simple ideological cliché. The school is a failure, they tell us, without giving us a deeper understanding of what the schools have and have not accomplished. Bureaucracy is antihumanistic and unnecessary, they agree, without providing an analysis that would enable us to control and redirect the bureaucratic process, whose reach is enlarged by every new demand for governmental services and regulation.

By contrast, a political analysis of educational history asks a series of open-ended, empirical questions: How was education policy made? What educational issues were involved? Who participated? What was their self-interest and how did they perceive it? How were the issues resolved? How did the participants try to influence the outcome? Who gained what? Who lost what? What alternatives were available? Why were they rejected? How did the press and other influential agencies affect the issue? How did the resolution of the issue affect the original problem? The questions could be multiplied; the important criterion is that the answer is not presumed by the question.

Politicized history, written in reaction to the mood of the moment, becomes dated as the mood of the moment fades. The most useful and most relevant approach to educational history is that which seeks to determine how ideas are translated into policy, how policy is translated into practice, how practice grows into policy, how schools respond or fail to respond to various kinds of aspirations, how families mediate their children's education, how social origins affect educational opportunity, and how political, social, and economic forces interrelate to affect the educational process. The possibilities for study are as boundless as the question of how knowledge, skills, values, and sensibilities are transmitted across time, across generations, and across cultures. An understanding of the democratic political process, a respect for rational inquiry, and a capacity for surprise are necessary equipment for those who attempt to reconstruct a sense of the past and to understand the role of education in it.

The point is that ideas have consequences. History matters, not only because of the importance of the search for knowledge, but because of the uses to which analyses of the past may be put. The interpretation of history can have political implications, and historians know this; they know that their readings of the past, especially when they delve into the origins and effects of contemporary social institutions, can influence public opinion and policymaking. By telling people who they are and what they have done and by telling a nation how its institutions have succeeded or failed, the historian helps us to define the limitations and possibilities of the present and future.

The historian who undertakes to demonstrate that kindergartens and vocational education were intended to "oppress" and "contain" the children of the poor directs his message at present policymakers. The historian who maintains that American rhetoric and American reality are not only far apart but are entirely contradictory has a political purpose, which is not to encourage people to close the gap but to persuade them that the gap can never be closed because American society is inherently flawed. The historian who asserts that reform in American society always fails and that reformers have always been either knaves or fools is in reality insisting on the futility of reform. These are political messages, intended to have a political effect.

Consider the impact of historians who have argued that the "real" purpose of schools is not the cultivation of intelligence but social sorting, and that the "real" value of a degree is not what it represents in terms of learning but what it signifies in the competition for status. These are claims that became self-fulfilling prophecies because they encouraged educators to think of schools as degree-granting custodial institutions. One consequence for policymaking has been to justify a decline in educational standards, as evidenced by policies of automatic promotion in elementary and secondary schools, and at the postsecondary level, by the acceptance of grade inflation, diploma mills, and term-paper factories. These changes did not come about solely because of the way history has been written in recent years, but the repeated assertions by historians and social scientists that schooling was of little or no intrinsic value has had its impact on policymakers.

To the extent that history influences social policy, it should be to enable policymakers to understand the complexity of events and institutions and the tenuousness of causal connections. In the light of historical analysis, the assertion that schools end crime and poverty is as simplistic and naive as the claim that the schools maintain inequality. (There is an unfortunate evangelistic tone to educational commentary that leads to either excessive acclamation or excessive denunciation.) Thus, the old belief in the school as the great panacea has been replaced by the opposite belief either that the school is utterly impotent and ineffective, or that it is an evil, all-powerful mechanism of social stratification and technological blight. We know from experience that crime and poverty have survived the widespread extension of schooling; we also know that schooling has enabled many people to rise above their social origins and that advanced technology produces not just bombs and pollutants but also the means to cure disease and avert famine. It *is* possible to see American history as something other than a road map to heaven or hell.

If the evangelistic tradition were set aside, then perhaps schools might be understood neither as the single institution most responsible for America's greatness nor as the single institution most responsible for its ills. It might, perhaps, be possible to think of schools in terms that are modest and reasonable and that are appropriately related to their capacities. Seen in this light, the American schoolteacher might emerge as neither a miracle worker of superhuman dimensions nor as an agent of malevolent forces, but as a rather ordinary citizen with a complicated job to do.

Suppose, for the sake of discussion, that schools do not have cosmic purposes; that they cannot "save" society; that they are neither spearheads of radical change nor instruments of cultural repression. Think instead of institutions whose purposes are circumscribed by the public that supports them, and whose goals are limited and potentially attainable. Universal literacy is one such goal that, despite the massive expansion of schooling both vertically and horizontally, has not yet been achieved; universal access to higher education is another such goal which, with the recent burgeoning of public institutions, has become a virtual reality.

But even universal literacy and universal access to the highest levels of schooling do not solve larger social problems. People with equal amounts of schooling do not earn equal incomes nor does high educational attainment safeguard the degree-bearer against economic misfortune, mental instability, social insecurity, or life's other travails. Education does not guarantee success, however it is defined, but it does offer opportunity. How that opportunity is used depends to a very great extent on the ability and motivation of the individual. This is not to deny the importance of the social and economic problems which are not solved by schooling, but to suggest that they might be more directly and fruitfully attacked in noneducational ways.

Education in a liberal society must sustain and hold in balance ideals that coexist in tension: equality and excellence. While different generations have emphasized one or the other, in response to the climate of the times, schools alone cannot make either ideal a reality, though they contribute to both. The schools are limited institutions which have certain general responsibilities and certain specific capacities; sometimes they have failed to meet realistic expectations, and at other times they have succeeded beyond realistic expectations in dispersing intelligence and opportunity throughout the community. In order to judge them by reasonable standards and in order to have any chance of improving their future performance, it is necessary to abandon the simplistic search for heroes and devils, for scapegoats and panaceas.

NOTES

CHAPTER ONE

1. Richard Hofstadter, *Anti-intellectualism in American Life* (New York: Random House, Vintage Books, 1962), p. 301.

2. Merle Curti, *The Social Ideas of American Educators* (1935; reprinted ed., Totowa, N.J.: Littlefield, Adams, 1971), p. 125; John Dewey, *Freedom and Culture* (New York: G. P. Putnam's Sons, 1939), p. 42.

3. Dewey, *Freedom and Culture*, pp. 39–40.

4. Albert Fishlow, "The American Common School Revival: Fact or Fancy?" in *Industrialism in Two Systems*, ed. Henry Rosovsky (New York: John Wiley & Sons, 1966), pp. 40–66.

5. Carl L. Becker, *New Liberties for Old* (New Haven: Yale University Press, 1941), p. 151.

CHAPTER TWO

1. R. Jackson Wilson, "United States: The Reassessment of Liberalism," in *The New History*, ed. Walter Laqueur and George L. Mosse (New York: Harper Torchbooks, 1966), pp. 90–102.

2. Bernard Bailyn, *Education in the Forming of American Society* (Chapel Hill, N.C.: University of North Carolina Press, 1960), pp. 5–9.

3. Ibid., pp. 8–14, 53.

4. Lawrence A. Cremin, *The Wonderful World of Ellwood Patterson Cubberley* (New York: Teachers College Press, 1965), pp. 2, 6.

5. Ibid., pp. 11–12.

6. Ibid., pp. 13, 22.

7. Ibid., pp. 43, 46–47; Lawrence A. Cremin, "The Curriculum Maker and His Critics: A Persistent American Problem," *Teachers College Record* 54 (1952–53): 234; Lawrence A. Cremin, *American Education: The Colonial Experience, 1607–1783* (New York: Harper & Row, 1970), p. x.

8. Bailyn, *Education in the Forming*, p. 14; Cremin, *American Education*, p. xi.

9. For a review of new work in educational historiography, see Douglas Sloan, "Historiography and the History of Education," in *Review of Research in Education*, ed. Fred N. Kerlinger (Itasco, Ill.: F. E. Peacock, 1973), 1: 239–269; for a critique of Bailyn and Cremin, see R. Freeman Butts, "Public Education and Political Community," *History of Education Quarterly*, Vol. 14, No. 2 (Summer 1974): 165–183.

10. Lawrence A. Cremin, *Traditions of American Education* (New York: Basic Books, 1977), p. 134.

11. Michael B. Katz, *The Irony of Early School Reform: Educational Innovation in Mid-Nineteenth Century Massachusetts* (Boston: Beacon Press, 1968); Michael B. Katz, *Class, Bureaucracy, and Schools: The Illusion of Educational Change in America* (New York: Praeger, 1971); Colin Greer, *The Great School Legend* (New York: Basic Books, 1972); Clarence Karier, *Shaping the American Educational State: 1900 to the Present* (New York: Free Press, 1975); Clarence Karier, Paul Violas, and Joel Spring, *Roots of Crisis: American Education in the Twentieth Century* (Chicago: Rand McNally, 1973); Joel Spring, *Education and the Rise of the Corporate State* (Boston: Beacon Press, 1972); Joel Spring, *A Primer of Libertarian Education* (New York: Free Life Editions, 1975); Walter Feinberg, *Reason and Rhetoric: The Intellectual Foundations of Twentieth Century Liberal Educational Policy* (New York: John Wiley & Sons, 1975); Walter Feinberg and Henry Rosemont, Jr., eds., *Work, Technology, and Education: Dissenting Essays in the Intellectual Foundations of American Education* (Urbana: University of Illinois Press, 1975); Samuel Bowles and Herbert Gintis, *Schooling in Capitalist America: Educational Reform and the Contradictions of Economic Life* (New York: Basic Books, 1976).

CHAPTER THREE

1. John Vaizey, ed., *Education: The State of the Debate in America, Britain, and Canada* (London: Duckworth, 1976), pp. 31–32; see also, John H. Bunzel, *Anti-Politics in America: Reflections on the Anti-Political Temper and Its Distortions of the Democratic Process* (New York: Alfred A. Knopf, 1967).

2. Bowles and Gintis (*Schooling in Capitalist America*, p. 230) include David Tyack, Carl Kaestle, and Marvin Lazerson as part of this radical strand of revisionism. While the work of these historians includes some of the radical themes, each has criticized central elements of the radical analysis. See, David Tyack, *The One Best System: A History of American Urban Education* (Cambridge: Harvard University Press, 1974), p. 10, for a critique of the radical interpretation of "social control" and "reform by imposition"; see, Carl F. Kaestle, "Social Reform and the Urban School," *History of Education Quarterly*, Summer 1972, p. 217, where he calls for a synthesis that goes beyond the premise that the school has been either an unqualified success or an unequivocal failure; and see, Marvin Lazerson, "Revisionism and American Educational History," *Harvard Educational Review* 43, no. 2 (1973): 282–283, where Lazerson warns that the radical historiography may turn out to be as static, as presentist, and as simplistic as the old historiography.

3. Lazerson, "Revisionism and American Educational History," p. 270.

4. For illustrative examples of these themes, see Katz, *The Irony of Early School Reform*, pp. 1, 50, 53, 86, 130–131; Katz, *Class, Bureaucracy, and Schools*, pp. xviii–xxiv, 39, 108–110, 115–116, 122; Karier, Violas, and

Spring, *Roots of Crisis*, pp. 3–4, 6–7, 9–12, 22, 39, 88; Karier, *Shaping the American Educational State*, pp. xx, 2–9, 138–139, 144; Greer, *The Great School Legend*, pp. 3–4, 33–56, 74–79, 109–111, 152; Spring, *Education and the Rise of the Corporate State*, pp. 1, 2, 72, 75, 87–89, 162–163. These themes are employed selectively by Feinberg and by Bowles and Gintis. See Feinberg, *Reason and Rhetoric*, pp. 39, 171–172, 197–199, 235–236; see also Feinberg's critique of the radical historians on pp. 236–262. See Bowles and Gintis, *Schooling in Capitalist America*, pp. 18–19, 27–30, 39, 186, 227, 234; for their critique of the radical historians, see pp. 235–241, 250–263.

5. In *Education and the Rise of the Corporate State* (pp. 100–103), Spring cites Counts's role as a radical critic, but both Counts and Curti are elsewhere criticized as liberals; see Karier, Violas, and Spring, *Roots of Crisis*, pp. 3–5; Karier, *Shaping the American Educational State*, pp. 4–5; and Feinberg, *Reason and Rhetoric*, pp. 100–103, 202–207.

6. Kaestle, "Social Reform and the Urban School," p. 216.

7. Katz, *The Irony of Early School Reform*, p. 1; Greer, *The Great School Legend*, p. 3; see also, Katz, *Class, Bureaucracy, and Schools*, pp. xxi, 123; Karier, Violas, and Spring, *Roots of Crisis*, pp. 2–5; Bowles and Gintis, *Schooling in Capitalist America*, pp. 225–230.

8. Sloan, "Historiography and the History of Education," pp. 247–248.

9. John E. Talbott, "Education in Intellectual and Social History," *Historical Studies Today*, ed. Felix Gilbert and Stephen R. Graubard (New York: W. W. Norton, 1972), pp. 195–196.

10. Karier, *Roots of Crisis*, pp. 11, 95–107; Violas, *Roots of Crisis*, pp. 66–83. For a radical view of Counts, see Feinberg, *Reasons and Rhetoric*, pp. 203–207.

11. Robert W. Hodge and Donald J. Treiman, "Class Identification in the United States," *American Journal of Sociology* 73, no. 5 (1968): 535–547.

12. Russell Marks, "Race and Immigration: The Politics of Intelligence Testing," in Karier, *Shaping the American Education State*, pp. 335–336; Rush Welter, "Reason, Rhetoric, and Reality in American Educational History," *The Review of Education* 2 (January/February 1976): 94–96; for an excellent critique of the functionalist approach, see David K. Cohen and Bella H. Rosenberg, "Functions and Fantasies: Understanding Schools in Capitalist America," *History of Education Quarterly*, Summer 1977.

13. For a survey of the ideology of vocationalism, see Marvin Lazerson and W. Norton Grubb, eds., *American Education and Vocationalism, A Documentary History, 1870–1970* (New York: Teachers College Press, 1974).

14. Katz, *Class, Bureaucracy, and Schools*, pp. xviii, xx, xxii–xxiii, xxiv, 108, 122. See also, Greer, *The Great School Legend*, pp. 72–76; Bowles and Gintis, *Schooling in Capitalist America*, pp. 55–56, 186, 192; Karier, *Roots of Crisis*, p. 126; Spring, *Roots of Crisis*, p. 143.

15. Katz, *Class, Bureaucracy, and Schools*, p. 9; Kaestle, "Social Reform and the Urban School," p. 214; Carl F. Kaestle, *The Evolution of an Urban School System: New York, 1750–1850* (Cambridge: Harvard University Press, 1973), p. 182.

16. Diane Ravitch, *The Great School Wars: New York City, 1805–1973* (New York: Basic Books, 1974), pp. 79–133; Katz, *Class, Bureaucracy, and Schools*, pp. 15, 20.

Notes

17. Katz, *Class, Bureaucracy, and Schools*, p. 22.

18. Harold Silver, "Aspects of Neglect: The Strange Case of Victorian Popular Education," *Oxford Review of Education* 3, no. 1 (1977): 57–69.

19. David C. Hammack, "The Centralization of New York City's Public School System, 1896: A Social Analysis of a Decision" (master's thesis, Columbia University, 1969); Ravitch, *The Great School Wars*, pp. 134–186; Spring, *Education and the Rise of the Corporate State*, pp. 85–90. Greer notes that the leadership of the newly centralized system passed rapidly from the Protestant reformers to the ethnic minorities (*The Great School Legend*, pp. 81–82).

20. Greer, *The Great School Legend*, p. 120; Spring, *Education and the Rise of the Corporate State*, pp. 62–90.

21. *New York Times*, 15 September 1897; Kate Holladay Claghorn, "The Foreign Immigrant in New York City," *United States Industrial Commission, Report on Immigration*, Vol. 15, 1900, pp. 449–92; Ravitch, *The Great School Wars*, pp. 179–180.

22. Ravitch, *The Great School Wars*, pp. 197–228.

23. Selwyn K. Troen, *The Public and the Schools: Shaping the St. Louis System, 1838–1920* (Columbia, Mo. University of Missouri Press, 1975), pp. 151, 224–226.

CHAPTER FOUR

1. Katz, *The Irony of Early School Reform*, pp. 214–215; Katz, *Class, Bureaucracy, and Schools*, pp. xviii–xxiv, 39–48, 108, 122; Karier, *Roots of Crisis*, pp. 12, 17, 84–107; Violas, *Roots of Crisis*, pp. 72–74.

2. Katz, *Class, Bureaucracy, and Schools*, p. 48.

3. Arnold H. Leibowitz, "Educational Policy and Political Acceptance: The Imposition of English as the Language of Instruction in American Schools" (Washington, D.C.: Center for Applied Linguistics, ERIC Clearinghouse for Linguistics, March 1971); John B. Shotwell, *A History of the Schools of Cincinnati* (Cincinnati, Ohio: School Life Co., 1902), pp. 289–301; Joshua A. Fishman, *Language Loyalty in the United States* (The Hague, Netherlands: Mouton & Co., 1966), p. 233; and Heinz Kloss, *Excerpts from the National Minority Laws of the United States of America* (Honolulu, Hawaii: East-West Center, 1966), pp. 48–55.

4. David Tyack, "The Perils of Pluralism: The Background of the Pierce Case," *American Historical Review* 74 (October 1968): 74–98; Pierce v. Society of Sisters, 268 U.S. 510 (1925).

5. Meyer v. Nebraska, 262 U.S. 390 (1923); Leibowitz, "Educational Policy," p. 34.

6. Theodore Andersson and Mildred Boyer, *Bilingual Schooling in the United States* (Washington, D.C.: U.S. Government Printing Office, 1970), p. 211; Robert F. Berkhofer, Jr., *Salvation and the Savage: An Analysis of Protestant Missions and American Indian Response, 1787–1862* (New York: Atheneum, 1972), pp. 16–43; Leibowitz, "Educational Policy," pp. 67–78; U.S. Senate Committee on Labor and Public Welfare, Special Subcommittee on Indian Education, *Indian Education: A National Tragedy—A*

National Challenge (Washington, D.C.: U.S. Government Printing Office, 1969), pp. 147–148; G. E. E. Lindquist, *The Red Man in the United States* (New York: George H. Doran, 1923) , pp. 40–41; Institute for Government Research, *The Problems of Indian Administration* (Baltimore: Johns Hopkins Press, 1928), pp. 22, 403–412.

7. Carter G. Woodson, *The Education of the Negro Prior to 1861* (Washington, D.C.: Associated Publishers, 1919), pp. 1, 128–144, 205–208; Henry Allen Bullock, *A History of Negro Education in the South: From 1619 to the Present* (Cambridge, Mass.: Harvard University Press, 1967), pp. 5–15, 21–26, 57–58.

8. Thomas Sowell, "Three Black Histories," *American Ethnic Groups* (Washington, D.C.: The Urban Institute, 1978), p. 17.

9. Horace Mann Bond, *Black American Scholars: A Study of Their Beginnings* (Detroit, Michigan: Balamp Publishing, 1972), pp. 23, 53.

10. Thomas Sowell, "Black Excellence: The Case of Dunbar High School," *The Public Interest*, no. 35 (Spring 1974), pp. 3–21.

11. Theodore Dreiser, *Dawn* (New York: Horace Liveright, 1931), pp. 129–131, 190–192.

12. Timothy L. Smith, "Immigrant Social Aspirations and American Education, 1880–1930," *American Quarterly* 21, no. 3 (Fall 1969): 523–543; Jane Addams, *Newer Ideals of Peace* (Chautauqua, N.Y.: Chautauqua Press, 1907), p. 77.

13. John Walker Briggs, "Italians in Italy and America: A Study of Change within Continuity for Immigrants to Three American Cities, 1890–1930" (Ph.D. diss., University of Minnesota, 1973), pp. 258–285; Mordecai Soltes, *The Yiddish Press: An Americanizing Agency* (New York: Teachers College Press, 1925), pp. 151–152.

14. Heinz Kloss, *National Minority Laws*, pp. 48–55.

15. Joshua A. Fishman, *Language Loyalty*, pp. 29–30, 233.

CHAPTER FIVE

1. Spring, *Roots of Crisis*, p. 143; Katz, *The Irony of Early School Reform*, pp. 90–91; Greer, *The Great School Legend*, pp. 93, 99, 109; Bowles and Gintis, *Schooling in Capitalist America*, pp. 8, 85; Karier, *Shaping the American Educational State*, p. 2.

2. Stephan Thernstrom, *Poverty and Progress: Social Mobility in a Nineteenth Century City* (Cambridge: Harvard University Press, 1964), p. 1.

3. Ibid., pp. 96–103, 154–156, 161.

4. Ibid., pp. 114, 164–165.

5. William Miller, "American Historians and the Business Elite," in *Men in Business: Essays on the Historical Role of the Entrepreneur*, ed. William Miller (New York: Harper Torchbooks, 1962), pp. 309–328; also, Frances W. Gregory and Irene D. Neu, "The American Industrial Elite in the 1870s: Their Social Origins," in *Men in Business*, pp. 193–212.

6. Herbert G. Gutman, "The Reality of the Rags-to-Riches 'Myth': The Case of the Paterson, New Jersey, Locomotive, Iron, and Machinery

Notes

Manufacturers, 1830–1880," in *Nineteenth Century Cities: Essays in the New Urban History*, ed. Stephan Thernstrom and Richard Sennett (New Haven: Yale University Press, 1969), pp. 121–122.

7. Clyde Griffen, "Workers Divided: The Effect of Craft and Ethnic Differences in Poughkeepsie, New York, 1850–1880," in *Nineteenth Century Cities*, pp. 58–59, 92–93.

8. Paul B. Worthman, "Working Class Mobility in Birmingham, Alabama, 1880–1914," in *Anonymous Americans: Explorations in Nineteenth, Century Social History*, ed. Tamara K. Hareven (Englewood Cliffs, New Jersey: Prentice-Hall, 1971), pp. 193–197.

9. Richard J. Hopkins, "Status, Mobility, and the Dimensions of Change in a Southern City, Atlanta, 1870–1910," in *Cities in American History*, ed. Kenneth T. Jackson and Stanley K. Schultz (New York: Alfred A. Knopf, 1972), pp. 221–222.

10. Michael P. Weber, *Social Change in an Industrial Town, Patterns of Progress in Warren, Pennsylvania, from Civil War to World War I* (University Park, Pennsylvania: Pennsylvania State University, 1976), pp. 54–56.

11. Thomas Kessner, *The Golden Door: Italian and Jewish Immigrant Mobility in New York City, 1880–1915* (New York: Oxford University Press, 1977), pp. 162–163, 170–171; for a comparison of several cities' mobility rates, see Stephan Thernstrom, *The Other Bostonians: Poverty and Progress in the American Metropolis, 1880–1970* (Cambridge: Harvard University Press, 1973), p. 234. For another fascinating discussion of the relationship between education and social mobility for certain immigrant groups, see Josef J. Barton, *Peasants and Strangers: Italians, Rumanians, and Slovaks in an American City, 1890–1950* (Cambridge: Harvard University Press, 1975).

12. Stephan Thernstrom, "Reflections on the New Urban History," in *Historical Studies Today*, ed. Felix Gilbert and Stephen R. Graubard (New York: W. W. Norton, 1972), p. 329.

13. Thernstrom, *The Other Bostonians*, p. 4.

14. Ibid., pp. 70–72.

15. Ibid., pp. 72–74, 91–94.

16. Ibid., p. 94.

17. Ibid., pp. 92–93.

18. Ibid., p. 232; Kessner, *The Golden Door*, pp. 132–136.

19. Thernstrom, *The Other Bostonians*, pp. 257–258.

20. Ibid., pp. 75, 258.

21. Katz, *Class, Bureaucracy, and Schools*, p. 121.

22. Greer, *The Great School Legend*, pp. 80, 83; David Tyack, "A Tract for the Times," *The Andover Review* 1, no. 1 (1974): 135.

23. Bowles and Gintis, *Schooling in Capitalist America*, p. 110.

24. Thernstrom, *The Other Bostonians*, pp. 56, 72, 76; Katz, *Class, Bureaucracy, and Schools*, introduction by Stephan Thernstrom.

25. Peter M. Blau and Otis Dudley Duncan, *The American Occupational Structure* (New York: John Wiley & Sons, 1967), pp. 77–78.

26. Ibid., p. 157.

27. Ibid., p. 201.

28. Ibid., pp. 432–435.

29. Ibid., p. 113; *The Big Business Executive 1964: A Study of His Social and Educational Background*, sponsored by *Scientific American*, conducted by Market Statistics Inc. of New York City, in collaboration with Dr. Mabel Newcomer and updating Mabel Newcomer, *The Big Business Executive— The Factors That Made Him: 1900–1950* (New York: Columbia University Press, 1950), cited in Seymour Martin Lipset's "Equality and Inequality," in *Contemporary Social Problems*, 4th ed., ed. Robert Merton and Robert Nisbet (New York: Harcourt, Brace, Jovanovich, 1976), p. 319.

30. Christopher Jencks et al., *Inequality: A Reassessment of the Effect of Family and Schooling in America* (New York: Basic Books, 1972), pp. 7–8, 176, 179, 181, 185, 191, 196.

31. For the debate, see Daniel Bell, "Meritocracy and Equality," *The Public Interest*, no. 29 (Fall 1972), pp. 29–68; Daniel Bell, *The Cultural Contradictions of Capitalism* (New York: Basic Books, 1976), pp. 260–274; James S. Coleman et al., *Equality of Educational Opportunity* (Washington: U.S. Government Printing Office, 1966); Frederick Mosteller and Daniel Patrick Moynihan, eds., *On Equality of Educational Opportunity* (New York: Random House, 1972); John Rawls, *A Theory of Justice* (Cambridge: Harvard University Press, 1971); Robert Nisbet, "The Pursuit of Equality," *The Public Interest*, no. 35 (Spring 1974), pp. 103–120; Arthur M. Okun, *Equality and Efficiency: The Big Tradeoff* (Washington, D.C.: Brookings Institution, 1975).

CHAPTER SIX

1. Blau and Duncan, *The American Occupational Structure*, p. 233.

2. Andrew M. Greeley, "The Ethnic Miracle," *The Public Interest*, no. 45 (Fall 1976), pp. 20–36.

3. Blau and Duncan, *The American Occupational Structure*, pp. 209–210.

4. Ibid., pp. 210–212.

5. Bowles and Gintis, *Schooling in Capitalist America*, p. 6; Karier, *Shaping the American Education State*, p. 408; see also, Feinberg, *Reason and Rhetoric*, pp. 22–23, 163–164.

6. Karier, *Shaping the American Educational State*, pp. xvi, 281; W. Vance Grant and C. George Lind, *Digest of Educational Statistics* (Washington: U.S. Government Printing Office, 1975), p. 152.

7. U.S. Department of Commerce, Bureau of the Census, *The Social and Economic Status of the Black Population in the United States, 1974* (Washington: U.S. Government Printing Office, 1974), pp. 14–15, 150–154.

8. Ibid., pp. 13–14.

9. Ibid., pp. 27, 42.

10. Ibid., pp. 37–43.

11. Ralph W. Tyler, "The Federal Role in Education," *The Public Interest*, no. 34 (Winter 1974), p. 170; Alex Inkeles, "Review of the International Evaluation of Educational Achievement," *Proceedings of the National Academy of Education* 4 (1977): 185–186.

Notes

12. See the following titles in U.S. Bureau of the Census, *Current Population Reports*: Series P-20, no. 272, 278, 294, 309, "School Enrollment—Social and Economic Characteristics of Students"; Series P-20, no. 307, "Population Characteristics—Population Profile of the United States, 1976," p. 18; Series P-23, no. 54, "The Social and Economic Status of the Black Population in the United States, 1974," p. 95. See also, "Black College Enrollment Held Equal to Population Proportion," *New York Times*, 4 December 1975, p. 33.

13. Richard B. Freeman, *Black Elite: The New Market for Highly Educated Black Americans* (New York: McGraw-Hill, 1977).

14. Ibid., p. 27.

15. Ibid., pp. 34–36.

16. Ibid., pp. 30–34, 19–25.

17. Ibid., pp. 30–39.

18. Ibid., pp. 37–38.

19. Ibid., pp. 38, 53.

20. Ibid., pp. 23, 47, 58–59, 95–96; Blau and Duncan, *The American Occupational Structure*, pp. 210–212.

21. Robert M. Hauser and David L. Featherman, "Occupations and Social Mobility in the United States," speech delivered at the American Association for the Advancement of Science meeting in Boston, Mass., February 1976; idem, "Socioeconomic Achievements of U.S. Men, 1962–1972," *Science*, 26 July 1974, pp. 325–331.

22. David L. Featherman, "Schooling and Social Mobility in Modern America," speech delivered at Franklin and Marshall College, March 1, 1976.

23. Ibid.

24. Lipset, "Equality and Inequality," pp. 328–329.

CHAPTER SEVEN

1. Katz, *The Irony of Early School Reform*, pp. 218, 112.

2. Ibid., pp. 148–151.

3. Ibid., pp. 151–152.

4. Ibid., pp. 216–217; see also, Wayne J. Urban, "A Philosophical Critique of Michael Katz's Educational History," *Proceedings of the Philosophy of Education Society*, 1973, ed. Brian Crittenden, pp. 94–103.

5. Katz, *The Irony of Early School Reform*, pp. 53, 84.

6. Ibid., pp. 20, 273. Katz's description of a "significant majority" of businessmen in favor of the high school refers to an erroneous total on page 273. Katz mistotaled the "votes to abolish" among businessmen; instead of 24 against the high school, as he has it, the actual total of his figures is 28. Thus, instead of a "business" vote of 30–24 in favor of the high school, the actual vote was 30–28 in favor (and four of the votes *for* the school were cast by "business employees").

7. Ibid., pp. 84, 273.

8. Ibid., p. 86; Alice Felt Tyler, *Freedom's Ferment: Phases of American Social History to 1860* (Minneapolis: University of Minnesota Press, 1944), p. 233; Ellwood P. Cubberley, *Public Education in the United States*, rev. ed. (Boston: Houghton Mifflin, 1947), pp. 164–165; Lawrence A. Cremin, *The American Common School* (New York: Teachers College Press, 1951), pp. 29, 47, 92; Sidney Jackson, *America's Struggle for Free Schools* (Washington: American Council on Public Affairs, 1942); Merle Curti, *The Social Ideas of American Educators* (New York: Scribner's, 1935). According to Katz's figures, there were 129 votes cast favoring the high school, including 32 (or 24.8 percent) by shoemakers, mariners, and fishermen; 37 (or 28.6 percent) by artisans and farmers (p. 273).

9. Katz, *The Irony of Early School Reform*, pp. 19, 31, 26–27.

10. Ibid., p. 218.

11. Katz, *Class, Bureaucracy, and Schools*, p. 139.

12. Katz, *The Irony of Early School Reform*, p. 149.

13. Karier, Violas, and Spring, *Roots of Crisis*, pp. 3–5.

14. Ibid., pp. 1–5.

15. Lawrence A. Cremin, *The Transformation of the School: Progressivism in American Education, 1876–1957* (New York: Alfred A. Knopf, 1961), p. viii; Kaestle, "Social Reform and the Urban School," p. 216.

16. Karier, *Roots of Crisis*, pp. 91–92; Feinberg, *Reason and Rhetoric*, pp. 103–108.

17. Charles L. Zerby, "John Dewey and the Polish Question: A Response to the Revisionist Historians," *History of Education Quarterly* 15 (Spring 1975): 20; J. Christopher Eisele, "John Dewey and the Immigrants," *History of Education Quarterly* 15 (Spring 1975); 75.

18. Paul Violas, "Jane Addams and the New Liberalism," *Roots of Crisis*, pp. 70–73. Wayne J. Urban has expressed similar concerns about Violas's essay in "Some Historiographical Problems in Revisionist Educational History: Review of *Roots of Crisis*," *American Educational Research Journal* 12, no. 3 (Summer 1975) ; 339–340.

19. Jane Addams, *Democracy and Social Ethics* (New York: Macmillan, 1902), pp. 77–86; Violas, *Roots of Crisis*, p. 72.

20. Violas's mysterious footnote refers to Jane Addams, *The Spirit of Youth and the City Streets* (New York: Macmillan, 1909), p. 141; her typical views on ethic groups follow on pp. 143–145 and also on 100–102; Jane Addams, *Newer Ideals of Peace* (New York: Macmillan, 1907), p. 47.

21. Violas, *Roots of Crisis*, p. 77; Addams, *Newer Ideals of Peace*, p. 100.

22. Addams, *Spirit of Youth*, pp. 95–103; Violas, *Roots of Crisis*, p. 81.

23. Karier, *Shaping the American Educational State*, pp. xxii, 190, 276.

24. John Dewey, "Mediocrity and Individuality," *New Republic*, 6 December 1922, pp. 35–37; "Individuality, Equality, and Superiority," *New Republic*, 13 December 1922, pp. 61–63.

25. Karier, *Shaping the American Educational State*, pp. xv, 316–342.

26. Greer, *The Great School Legend*, pp. 105–129.

27. John Walker Briggs, "Italians in Italy and America," pp. 307–317; Greer, pp. 74–75.

28. Feinberg, *Reason and Rhetoric*, p. 133; see Wayne J. Urban, *Harvard Educational Review* 45, no. 4 (November 1975): 557.

Notes

29. Feinberg, *Reason and Rhetoric*, pp. 108–111; see *The Modern School Journal* for 1917 for its list of recommended reading in each issue.

30. Feinberg, *Reason and Rhetoric*, p. 243; John Dewey, "Conscience and Compulsion," *New Republic*, 14 July 1917, pp. 297–298.

31. Welter, "Reason, Rhetoric, and Reality," pp. 95–96.

32. James D. Anderson, "Education as a Vehicle for the Manipulation of Black Workers," in Feinberg and Rosemont, Jr., eds., *Work, Technology, and Education*, pp. 15–18.

33. Louis Harlan, *Separate and Unequal: Public School Campaigns and Racism in the Southern Seaboard States, 1901–1915* (Chapel Hill: University of North Carolina Press, 1958), pp. 78–80, 92–95, 100, 138, 254–255, 268–269.

34. Henry A. Bullock, *A History of Negro Education in the South* (Cambridge: Harvard University Press, 1967), pp. 100, 76, 88–89; Horace Mann Bond, *The Education of the Negro in the American Social Order* (1934; reprinted ed., New York: Octagon Books, 1966), pp. 55, 123–125, 131–132, 141–142, 149–150.

35. Anderson, "Education as a Vehicle," p. 35; Edgar Gardner Murphy, *Problems of the Present South* (New York: Macmillan, 1904), pp. 163–164.

36. Anderson, "Education as a Vehicle," p. 25; United States Senate, *Report of the Committee on Education and Labor Upon the Relations Between Labor and Capital* (Washington: U.S. Government Printing Office, 1885), vol. 4, pp. 772–781.

37. Bowles and Gintis, *Schooling in Capitalist America*, pp. 8, 13–14, 11, 123, 56, 103.

38. Ibid., pp. 14, 46, 60, 54, 55.

39. Ibid., pp. 62, 276, 265.

40. Ibid., pp. 266, 280, 287, 252.

41. William H. Sewell, "Inequality of Opportunity for Higher Education," *American Sociological Review* 36 (October 1971): 798; Robert M. Hauser and David L. Featherman, "Equality of Access to Schooling: Trends and Prospects," Center for Demography and Ecology, Working Paper 75-17, University of Wisconsin at Madison, 1975, pp. 20–21; see also, William H. Sewell and Robert M. Hauser, *Education, Occupation, and Earnings: Achievement in the Early Career* (New York: Academic Press, 1975), p. 184. In Sewell and Hauser's model, the inheritance of status positions across generations explains "no more than 16% of the variance in educational attainment, 12% of the variance in occupational status, and 4% of the variance in earnings."

42. Mervyn Matthews, "Soviet Students—Some Sociological Perspectives," *Soviet Studies* 27, no. 1 (January 1975); 86–108; Mervyn Matthews, *Class and Society in Soviet Russia* (New York: Walker, 1972), pp. 269–287; *New York Times*, 2 September 1977, p. 1; Ibid., 22 October 1977, p. 1.

43. Okun, *Equality and Efficiency*, p. 69; Simon Kuznets, "Demographic Aspects of the Distribution of Income Among Families: Recent Trends in the United States," *Econometrics and Economic Theory: Essays in Honor of Jan Tinbergen* (White Plains, N.Y.: International Arts and Sciences Press, 1974), pp. 223–245; Morton Paglin, "The Measurement and Trend of Inequality: A Basic Revision," *American Economic Review* 65,

no. 4 (September 1975): 602, 606–607; *New York Times*, 18 January 1977, p. 10.

44. U.S. Bureau of the Census, *Current Population Reports*, Series P-60, no. 107, "Money Income and Poverty Status of Families and Persons in the United States: 1976," (Washington, D.C.: U.S. Government Printing Office, 1977), p. 11.

45. Bowles and Gintis, *Schooling in Capitalist America*, pp. 183, 238.

46. Joel H. Spring, "Anarchism and Education: A Dissenting Tradition," *Roots of Crisis*, p. 217.

47. Spring, *Education and the Rise of the Corporate State*, pp. 1, 2, 3–21.

48. Ibid., pp. 49, 56–57, 76, 66–90.

49. Ibid., p. 94.

50. Joel H. Spring, *A Primer of Libertarian Education* (New York: Free Life Editions, 1975), pp. 82, 113, 115, 124–126, 137–138, 100.

51. Ibid., p. 21; William Godwin, *An Enquiry Concerning Political Justice and Its Influence on General Virtue and Happiness*, vol. 2, ed. Raymond A. Preston (New York: Alfred A. Knopf, 1926, p. 139).

52. Francisco Ferrer, *The Origin and Ideals of the Modern School* (New York: Putnam, 1913), pp. 11, 52–53; Spring, *Education and the Rise of the Corporate State*, pp. 67–68.

53. Spring, *Education and the Rise of the Corporate State*, pp. 64, 145; Joseph J. Cohen and Alexis C. Ferm, *The Modern School at Stelton* (Stelton, N.J.: Modern School Association, 1925), pp. 11, 44.

54. Cohen and Ferm, *The Modern School*, p. 65.

55. Joel H. Spring, *The Sorting Machine: National Educational Policy since 1945* (New York: McKay, 1976); Rita Kramer, *Maria Montessori* (New York: Putnam, 1976) , pp. 227–230.

CHAPTER EIGHT

1. David Hackett Fischer, *Historians' Fallacies: Toward a Logic of Historical Thought* (New York: Harper & Row, 1970), p. 314.

2. Karier, Violas, and Spring, *Roots of Crisis*, p. 5; Katz, *Class, Bureaucracy, and Schools*, pp. xxv, 106; Karier, *Shaping the American Educational State*, p. xxii; Sol Cohen, "The History of Urban Education in the United States: Historians of Education and Their Discontents," in *Urban Education in the Nineteenth Century*, ed. David A. Reeder (London: Taylor and Francis, 1977).

3. Hofstadter, *Anti-intellectualism in American Life*, p. 301.

INDEX

Index

Index

Halsey, Bishop, 145–46
Hammack, David C., 52
Harlan, Louis, 143–44
Hauser, Robert M., 112–14, 149
Hawaii, 61
Herrnstein, Richard, 90
Hierarchy, 147–48, 154
High schools, black, 66–67
History, American, *see* American history
History of education (educational historiography), 11–13, 21–28; black, 63–68; cultural transfer, 21–23, 26–27; institutional, 23, 24, 26–28; policy implications of, 169–71; politicization of, 165–70; profession of education glorified by, 21–23; radical revisionist, *see* Radical revisionism; states encouraged to prepare (1876), 24; *see also specific topics*
History of Education, A (Davidson), 22
Hofstadter, Richard, 4, 20, 168
Hopkins, Richard J., 81

Immigrants: Americanization of, 68–70; Gary plan and, 54–55; vocational education for, 46–47; *see also specific immigrant groups*
Income: of black college graduates, 110–11; of white minorities, 101
Income equality, 96–99
Income inequality, Bowles and Gintis on, 151–53
Indianapolis, Ind., 60
Individualism, 9, 14, 156
Industrial education, *see* Vocational education
Inequality (Jencks), 93–95
Inkeles, Alex, 106–7
Institutional analysis, radical, 41, 50
Institutional history of education, 23, 24, 26–28
Intentions of reformers, radical critique of, 41, 44–46, 50–52

International Evaluation of Educational Achievement, 106
Irish Catholics, 14, 53; income of, 101
Irish workers, social mobility of, 77, 79–80
Irony of Early School Reform, The: Educational Innovation in Mid-Nineteenth Century Massachusetts (Katz), 29, 116–26; as anti-activist, 125–26; Beverly, Mass., vote against high school, 119–22; participatory democracy, 125, 126; political process inadequately covered in, 118–19, 123; "reform by imposition," 117, 120, 125–26; soft-line vs. hard-line educators in, 118–19; working-class vs. radical goals, 124–25
Italians: alleged failure of, 138; Americanization of, 70; income of, 101; social mobility of, 82

Jackson, Sidney, 123
Japanese private schools in Hawaii, 61
Jefferson, Thomas, 9, 11, 13
Jencks, Christopher, 93–97, 106
Jews: Americanization of, 69, 70; demand for public schooling by, 54; income of, 101; social mobility of, 82–83
Johnson, Lyndon B., 33; "Great Society" programs of, 102–5
Justice, 139

Kaestle, Carl, 38, 48, 128
Karier, Clarence, 36, 42–43, 57–58, 127–30, 137–38; on blacks' prospects, 103; on Dewey, 129; on mobility, 74
Katz, Michael B., 29, 39, 57; on bureaucracy, class bias, and racism, 47–48; presentism of, 166–67; on social mobility, 74, 88;

Index